It's Conceivable!

Hypnosis for Fertility

2ND Edition

Lynsi Eastburn

ON THE COVER

LIAM GREY was conceived naturally after his Mom, Amber Olson, sought out Lynsi Eastburn's assistance. After the failure of several ART techniques over the course of three years, having endured emotional and financial devastation, yet *knowing there was a baby there*, Amber booked a private hypnotherapy session with Lynsi. She became pregnant after just two HypnoFertility® (HF) sessions and continued to see Lynsi for additional support throughout her pregnancy. Amber used Lynsi's fertility-specific birthing hypnosis (designed for women who have endured the trauma of infertility) protocol and gave birth to her darling little son naturally—and exactly on his due date, as it turned out. Liam is a *little-round-head* (a term Lynsi uses to describe the laidback demeanors of fertility/birth hypnosis babies)—truly as sweet and calm as he looks in his picture. Amber also worked with Lynsi to lose her pregnancy weight. She was so thrilled with her experience that less than a year after the birth of her son, Amber signed up for training at the innovative Eastburn Hypnotherapy Clinic & Institute, became a Certified HypnoFertility® Therapist, and—until her second HF baby, Devak, arrived just two years later—worked full-time at the clinic assisting other women in realizing their dreams of having a baby.

EDANA "EDIE" HARRIS (back cover) is one of Lynsi's HF babies too. Edie's mother, Jen, had suffered eleven years of infertility before she met Lynsi. By that time, she was doubtful that anything could help her to conceive. Jen had *known* her babies—a girl and a boy—since she was a young girl. She just couldn't understand why she could not have them. Edie was conceived naturally not long after Jen began the HF process. Jen also continued her work with Lynsi for pregnancy and birth support. As happened with Amber, Jen conceived Edie's little brother, Evan, within two years of her little girl's birth.

THOUGH these HF kiddos are teenagers as I release the second edition of this book, I have elected to keep their adorable photos on the cover because they represent the pioneers that helped to establish this blessed concept so many years ago.

"People usually consider walking on water
or in thin air a miracle.
But I think the real miracle is
not to walk either on water or in thin air,
but to walk on earth.
Every day we are engaged in a miracle which we don't
even recognize: a blue sky, white clouds, green leaves,
the black, curious eyes of a child — our own two eyes.
All is a miracle."

— Thich Nhat Hanh

COPYRIGHT

It's Conceivable! Hypnosis for Fertility
by Lynsi Eastburn
1st Edition ©2006
2nd Edition ©2017

ISBN: 978-1723485800
Printed in the United States of America.

CreateSpace, Independent Publishing

Order this book online at www.amazon.com
or at major online book retailers.

For Information Contact:

HypnoFertility® International
Eastburn Hypnotherapy Clinic
7905 N. Zenobia St.
Westminster, CO 80030
303-424-2331
office@hypnofertility.com
office@hypnodenver.com

www.hypnofertility.com
www.spiritbabywhisperer.com
www.hypnodenver.com

DISCLAIMER

The Author Entities, hereinafter referred to as "AEs", are defined as, but not necessarily limited to, the author (Lynsi Eastburn), any Eastburn Hypnotherapy Clinic/Center or HypnoFertility® practice or location, any location of the Eastburn Institute of Hypnosis, all employees of any above author or entity, and any contractor, instructor, agent, heir, legal assign, or corporate sponsor of the above author or entity.

The AEs offer the material printed in this book only as an informational study. None of the contents of this book may be considered formal advice. Such material is to be considered a guideline, to be reviewed and/or approved by your doctor(s), mental health professionals and/or other licensed medical providers. It is the responsibility of each person who purchases this book, and each person who may read or encounter the contained material, to comply with locally applicable laws, and to seek professional advice in any health-related matter.

No claims are made by the AEs as to the fitness of the contents of this book for any specific use. No form of warranty, express or implied, is offered to any reader of this book, regardless of whether or not said reader is the original purchaser of the book. The accuracy and relevance of the material contained in this book are not guaranteed in any way, express or implied. The AEs are not obligated to inform readers of any changes to facts presented in this book. By opening this book, all readers agree to recognize that the facts in the covered subject matter will change periodically and represent the opinions of those reasonably accepted to be experts in various fields, whose opinions may be subject to controversy and disagreement. Updates to the material are not an obligation of the AEs.

In addition, the AEs are not responsible for damages that result to any person or entity outside of those who have read this book, even if said damages occur as a result of the use of information herein.

All readers are held by the terms of this disclaimer, made binding by possessing this book and/or by being directly or indirectly exposed to any part of its content, whether in writing, verbally, or through any other medium.

Should the AEs develop and offer any courses related to the material in this book, the above indemnity shall extend to such course, whether or not said course uses this book as part of the course material or is referenced in that course.

TABLE OF CONTENTS

FOREWORD

I frequently tell my patients that when one stops to consider the complexities of human reproduction, it's a miracle we exist at all! Truly! That a tiny oocyte the size of a grain of sand and a mature human sperm cell one hundred times smaller than the oocyte manage to find each other and combine to create a human child is one of the most amazing creations of the universe. These aren't the musings of a defeatist, quite the opposite. It is rather the still genuine awe of a physician who has seen thousands of these "miracles" occur.

We've found lots of ways to ensure that sperm and egg meet up—whether it's IUI, in a Petri dish, or through ICSI—but sometimes even that isn't enough. During my career as a fertility doctor, I have always been in search of that extra something that will make the stars align in my clients' favor. I discovered long ago that straight science simply wasn't enough on many levels. So many of my clients struggle without answers or explanation as to why they can't conceive or carry a child to term. This struggle has a physical, emotional, and financial toll that can throw even the most connected relationships into a tailspin. But the simple answer is often that we just don't know why.

There are infinite factors at work, and try as we might, they cannot all be controlled. Stress, diet, our daily environment, our immune systems, inflammation, physiology, ovarian reserve, AMH, sperm motility, sperm morphology, and the list goes on and on. Even in a controlled laboratory setting with optimum conditions, there are times when we just can't make it happen. Some are surprised to hear doctors admit that western science doesn't have all the answers. For all that we now know, there is still so much that we don't. But it's our job to look to other schools of thought and disciplines for alternate pathways to achieving our goal.

I believe the eastern or alternative therapies hold so much potential to help. Time and again, I have seen couples trying to get pregnant only find the results they are after with the assistance of alternative therapies like HypnoFertility®.

Similar to yoga, acupuncture, and massage, HypnoFertility® is a mind-body technique that is that extra assistance that helps couples go from dreaming about children to becoming parents. The power of the mind is extraordinary. We've known this for centuries. The great sages and spiritual masters understood this and wrote about it– Buddha, Aristotle, Marcus Aurelius, and more recently, James Allen, Napoleon Hill, and others. Finally, mainstream medicine is taking notice. There have been too many "miracles" to dismiss.

Fertility treatment has come a long way since 1978 when the world first heard the words "test-tube" baby, and they conjured up an image of something Frankensteinian. This ground-breaking procedure has become the gold standard for fertility doctors around the globe. Twenty years ago, we didn't consider diet, the immune system, inflammation, or the subconscious mind as potential fertility roadblocks. We now know they play a major role. Specialties like Reproductive Immunology are now part of the treatment protocol. I believe complementary and alternative therapies that have been so helpful should become part of the standard of care as well.

When I'm at a speaking engagement or not wearing scrubs, I'm frequently wearing a t-shirt that says "Believe" on the front. The message is so important, we sell them to clients. I am convinced that it is the power of belief that makes the difference between a success story and a client who is still struggling. For those who say, "Seeing is believing," I say, "Believing is seeing."

HypnoFertility® offers hope even when hope has run dry. I suggest anyone looking to conceive spend some time exploring Lynsi Eastburn's marvelous book. HypnoFertility® is the powerful tool hopeful moms and dads have been searching for.

— Robert J. Kiltz, M.D.
Founder and Director of CNY Fertility
Board Certified Reproductive
Endocrinologist/OB/GYN

PREFACE

This book was inspired in many ways by my two wonderful sons, Kelly and Dylan. They are grown now, but when I originally wrote this they were 16 and 11 years old. I love being a mother and am particularly grateful to be *their* mother. They are bright, creative, sensitive, kind, friendly… I could write a book just describing their attributes. The sheer force of the love I feel for my boys is incredible. Although I have accomplished many things in my life, it is in being their mother that I am the most satisfied, the most fulfilled.

I have encountered many people who have little interest in children, people who believe that the conception of any child could only have been by accident. I have heard people say that there are enough children in the world, so why waste time and energy on the creation of more? I don't agree with that. In fact, I strongly disagree. I believe there is always room for a wanted child, and I believe that ultimately all children are wanted. Perhaps not always by their birth parents, but certainly by the Ultimate Universal Creative Force which expresses them into existence.

It is in the faces of my boys that I am ever reminded of the gift that is motherhood. Not a single day goes by when I do not thank God for the privilege of knowing them and loving them, let alone being able to raise them and guide them. And with this privilege comes recognition and responsibility. I recognize that many people have not yet experienced the joy that comes of having a child. I realize that I have an inner knowing, and an ability to assist others in achieving their dreams, and therefore a responsibility.

I have loved many children throughout my life. I have two amazing nephews, Luke and Chris, whose lives I am privileged to be a part of. I have a dozen or so young men, and even a couple of girls, that I have collected along the way. These are my "adopted" children, friends of my sons' who call me Mom. I've helped them with homework, attended graduations, and been the trusted confidant when no one else would listen.

My husband, Drake, is yet another inspiration to me on my life's journey. He is not only a gifted hypnotherapist and author, but a man of exemplary nature. Never having had any children of his own, he welcomed my boys into his life with a warm and loving heart. We adore him.

I share my blessings with you so that you may know how dedicated I am to assisting you along your path. To be a mother is the greatest gift. I want this for you. I know how much it means.

Lynsi Eastburn
Brighton, CO
May 29, 2017

"I live for my sons. I would be lost without them."
—*Princess Diana*

ACKNOWLEDGMENTS

This book would not have been possible without the assistance and support of Martie O'Brien, best known around Eastburn Hypnotherapy as the *Office Goddess*. Certified as a hypnotherapist herself, Martie's many talents include editing and graphic design. Martie retired in 2014. She is greatly missed (though we do still see her) and her warmth and sincerity are forever appreciated by all.

The second edition of *It's Conceivable!* would NEVER have been completed had it not been for my wonderful friend and soul sister, Kari Bengtson. Kari has one of the most kind and loving hearts I have ever known. Having struggled with her own fertility issues for many years, Kari's depth of compassion for others with similar struggles is virtually unparalleled. Her sincere desire to help in any way she can has brought hope and support to so many women. I am truly blessed to have her in my world.

I'd also like to thank:

Rachel Cook—Assistant Extraordinaire—for all her help with client care, miscellaneous office management, and "nit-picky" (she said that) proofreading assistance. Rachel is an awesome Certified HypnoFertility® Therapist herself and sees clients at my Westminster office.

Barb Lundy for her quick and efficient editing skills and proofreading assistance.

Mary Casey for her support and assistance, including — but definitely not limited to — her phenomenal proofreading skills.

Philo Couch *A.K.A. the Computer Wizard*, for the cover design, inside layout, endless hours of production assistance, editing, attention to detail… and much more.

Amber Olson for contributing the cover photo of her adorable son, her willingness to share her story for the benefit of others, and for her professionalism, positive energy, and compassion.

Jennifer Harris for contributing the *I'm Gonna Be a Big Sister* back cover photo of her beautiful daughter, her willingness to share her story to inspire others, and all the ways she supports women in their desires to have a family. As of this writing, this big sister is now 14, and her little brother is almost 12. I am in touch with them to this day, and it is such a joy to see *my babies* grow up.

My original professional hypnotherapy instructor and guide, Arthur Leidecker, for his magnificent teaching style and thorough training, and his generous assistance and encouragement every step of the way, including some editing assistance with this book.

Dr. C. Scot Giles for believing in me right from the moment we met, for advising me along the way, for teaching me some of the most profound advanced hypnotism techniques, and for his endless support and encouragement.

Dr. Robert Kiltz (RE) of CNY Fertility Center in New York for his recognition and support of HypnoFertility®. Dr. Kiltz is a pioneer in utilizing a blend of Eastern/Western healing modalities for ultimate patient care and success. He believes that mindset is everything, and is a huge proponent of Reiki, acupuncture, massage, yoga, and other complementary and alternative healing modalities. Dr. Kiltz's foresight and unique outlook has contributed significantly to establishing mainstream acceptance of RE/CAM and has helped elevate HypnoFertility® to critical mass.

Dr. Mark Bush (RE) of Colorado's *Conceptions Reproductive Associates of Colorado* for his open-mindedness and acceptance and support of me, HypnoFertility®, and the value of hypnosis to support fertility issues.

Marie Mongan, creator of *HypnoBirthing® – the Mongan Method*, for immediately recognizing the value and need for HypnoFertility®, and for honoring me with the HypnoBirthing® Institute's *Education and Literature* award in 2005.

Dr. Jia Gottlieb of Boulder's *Still Mountain*, for his holistic approach to medicine and his support of me personally, my clients, and my work with hypnosis.

The National Guild of Hypnotists for recognition and support not only of HypnoFertility®, but also for their tireless promotion of hypnosis as a separate and distinct profession, and the ethical practice of hypnotism.

Dr. Annamarie Fidel-Rice, Sr. Peg Maloney, Dr. Blenda Crawford, Dr. Martin McGovern, and Julie Sheehan, LPC of Regis University for their invaluable assistance and support in the completion and publication of my research study *Hypnosis as a Viable Technique for Infertility (2016)*.

And especially my father, Garry Carter, whose sudden and tragic death less than two weeks after I learned I was pregnant with my eldest son prompted me to pursue mastery of the healing arts, including meditation and hypnosis.

> *"Before you were conceived, I wanted you.*
> *Before you were born, I loved you.*
> *Before you were here an hour, I would die for you.*
> *This is the miracle of life."*
> *— Maureen Hawkins*

INTRODUCTION

"Making the decision to have a child — it's momentous.
It is to decide forever
to have your heart go walking outside your body."
— Elizabeth Stone

If you've been drawn to this book, you probably feel you know more about pregnancy and infertility than most practicing medical specialists. Chances are you cry each time someone tells you they're pregnant, and you avoid baby showers at all costs. You wonder, *What's wrong with me? Why can't I have a baby?* You've changed your diet — you don't drink alcohol, smoke, eat gluten or sugar, or consume caffeine. You've tried every supplement, herbal, and homeopathic remedy — sometimes choking down a dozen or more in a day. You monitor your cervical mucous, and meticulously track your menstrual cycles. You can't get out of bed before recording your basal body temperature, and it seems you are constantly "peeing on sticks." And then there's the apps. As if there wasn't already enough to obsess over, now there are dozens of fertility apps designed to track everything from menstrual cycles to ovulation to mood swings to intercourse — and everything else in between. You're hyper-sensitive to every twinge in your body. You feel like you should own stock in the companies that make ovulation kits and home pregnancy tests.

The tumultuous roller coaster that is now your life has dropped you deep into despair and you're not even sure why. It all started one day… you and your partner excitedly decided to start "trying." It was fun at first, romantic even, but then each month the start of your period would dash your excitement, and before long, the worry began to set in. Before you knew it, you were so preoccupied with thoughts of conception that it was all you could talk about. There's a strain on your relationship now, barely perceptible, perhaps, but there.

Well-meaning but sometimes insensitive advice of friends or family has begun to wear on your nerves. And some of your friends will no longer look you in the eye. They stop talking when you enter a room, and you know that they're talking about you. They feel sorry for you, or they think you're overreacting. That if you'd only *relax* you wouldn't have this problem.

You set up an appointment with your doctor and she tells you not to worry about it. Focus on other areas of your life and let nature take its course. It's too soon to see a specialist. But as time goes on, even the doctor begins to become concerned. You've *Googled* infertility—and found that you have a number of symptoms and it is definitely possible that you could have any of these problems. You decide it's time to see a specialist.

You check with your insurance company to find out what infertility procedures they will cover—if any. Some fertility clinics run a credit check on you—immediately—before you are even allowed to book a consultation. The reality of this process sets in, and' what you've been through thus far is nothing compared to what is to come.

An infertility diagnosis in either partner answers some questions, but you were ill-prepared for the emotional impact. Terrible guilt for the afflicted party perhaps. Anger, rage, fear, devastation—depending on the diagnosis and medical options. Financial concerns and considerations… choices. It wasn't supposed to be like this.

For those whose diagnoses are medically treatable, there are protocols that must be followed which can be time-consuming, painful, and expensive. And the statistics are not all that great. Although a diagnosis of "unexplained infertility" may seem positive to some, to others it is perceived as a terrible blow: *if there's nothing physiologically wrong with me, there's nothing they can do.* However, from a hypnosis standpoint, there's a lot we can do—in either case.

I am a Board Certified Hypnotherapist and Instructor through the National Guild of Hypnotists (NGH), and the State of Colorado, and have been working with hypnosis to promote fertility for nearly two decades now. I have a master's degree in Depth Psychology, and a master's in English. I have studied the mind, the brain, human behavior, and personality typology extensively for years; and I continue to do so. Because of what I've experienced in my private practice, and because, initially, there was a lack of any comprehensive exploration or application of hypnosis/hypnotherapy to support or enhance fertility, I essentially had to start from scratch as I began working more and more frequently in this arena. I specialize in fertility hypnosis; it is what I do every day. I don't just dabble in it—I live it. And I love it.

I have created a program—HypnoFertility®—which is tailored hypnosis specifically for fertility, and I teach this program to therapists internationally. Those who have trained with me are Certified HypnoFertility® Therapists (CHFT). The work I do has evolved over the years (I expound on this in my second book, *The 3 Keys to Conception*, so I will not go into it here). This book—*It's Conceivable!*—is based on my firsthand clinical experience with clients, and details the hypnotic process for your understanding.

I did not set out to create this specialty though helping women to have babies is definitely dear to my heart. I can remember when I was a kid and the first "test tube baby" was born in England. I heard it on the radio, and my first thought was *Thank God, now every woman who wants a baby will be able to have one!* I don't know why that thought popped into the mind of a nine-year-old kid, but I always did have a sensitivity around women who so desperately wanted babies. With all my heart, I wanted these women to have their babies. That has not changed.

Helping women to get pregnant is incredibly rewarding work. I really don't think of it as work at all. As more and more of my clients became pregnant, despite sometimes treacherous odds, I knew that this was my calling. My purpose. My path. That I had to dedicate my life to it.

Hypnosis has long been renowned for its effectiveness with issues such as smoking cessation, irritable bowel syndrome, weight loss, and anxiety. Not to mention childbirth. But because there wasn't much scientific research on the topic, my babies kept being dismissed as anecdotal evidence. I knew then, and I know now, that there is more to it than that. The lack of research inspired me to do my own study (which you can find in the appendix if you'd like to read it).

I knew right from the start that hypnosis would help with fertility issues. And it does. Whether or not it is "proven" scientifically is not my concern. Research does not *prove* anything anyway. It *indicates*. The word *prove* is not an academically accepted term in regard to research.

My clients want babies, and they don't care whether these babies are anecdotal or not. Nor do I. I have helped a lot of women become pregnant. It's not something I do, or even something I take credit for. I am the facilitator. My goal is to help you get back on track, back in balance of mind, body, and spirit. Hypnosis is the tool.

My clients tell me: "I feel there is a baby there." I believe that. I believe you. I believe *in* you. The rest, as they say, is history. Or, for our purposes, *her*story. The babies don't care if anyone calls them anecdotal evidence. They're warm, they're pink, they have that heavenly smell…

The purpose of this book — the reason I wrote it so many years ago and am releasing a second edition now — is to let people know that there is another option. Unlike the world of weight loss where there are literally countless products and services available to explore, there are limited options open when it comes to conceiving a baby. This book was written to provide hope; to let people know that there *is* another option. It is not a self-hypnosis book, in that it is not designed to teach self-hypnosis techniques. There are plenty of wonderful books available on that topic. In this book you'll learn what hypnosis really is, and the many ways it can help with fertility issues.

The following chapters illustrate the efficacy of hypnosis, the strength and capacity of your own mind. The power of the mind is enormous, and hypnosis is the most direct and rapid route to unlocking its potential. As you read the client cases contained within these pages, you will gain insight into what is possible. I have come to think of hypnosis as *the missing link*.

See the appendix for further articles and research…

Chapter 1

HYPNOSIS CAN HELP

"You gain strength, courage and confidence by every experience in which you really stop to look fear in the face. You are able to say to yourself, 'I have lived through this horror. I can take the next thing that comes along.' You must do the thing you think you cannot do."
— Eleanor Roosevelt

Chances are, if you've been struggling with infertility issues you've been told to "just relax." And that has probably driven you crazy. In fact, you are, no doubt, tired of hearing those words; tired of people's insensitive, unwanted advice; tired of feeling out of control of your life; tired of feeling broken. You are not broken. Hypnosis can help.

Throughout this book I will use words you may have heard many times before: infertility; relax; think positive; stress; obsession; unexplained; broken... and many others. From a hypnotic standpoint words often take on a different meaning or interpretation. For the sake of healthy fertility, and overall balance, it is extremely helpful to learn to speak (and think) from a hypnotic standpoint. As you begin to integrate hypnotic languaging techniques you will find it quite amazing that words which once elicited a terrible, gut-wrenching response from you are now processed smoothly and effectively, while you remain calm and in *a balanced* control of yourself and your life.

Due to misunderstandings surrounding the word hypnosis you will find that some references to it have been disguised by terms such as guided imagery, creative visualization, or simply mind/body, or relaxation techniques. These modalities do, in fact, stem from hypnosis; however, hypnosis is much more than simple guided imagery or visualization. Relaxation techniques are very beneficial—they just are not always enough. Sometimes it takes more—and, if that is the case, a skilled hypnotherapist can make all the difference. This is vital information when you feel you need access to the most powerful techniques available. It can be, and often is, the difference between success and failure.

I deliberately use the word hypnosis to describe the work I do with fertility because this word denotes a potency that is just not available through diluted versions of the practice. I refer to my work as hypnosis for fertility or *HypnoFertility*®. The methods illustrated in the pages of this book are based on the program I created from years of working one-on-one with fertility clients in my private practice. Since I began teaching the certification course in 2003, I have trained well over a thousand Certified HypnoFertility® Therapists worldwide, who specifically practice the techniques in this book.

During my early years in private practice, I encountered women who had initially sought out my hypnotherapy services because they had a fear of needles that had been aggravated or intensified by the infertility procedures they had undergone or would need to undergo. Experiencing such a deep state of relaxation (pretty much a foreign concept for a woman dealing with traditional *in*fertility) during the initial hypnotherapy session, these clients elected time and again to continue the hypnotherapy sessions to support the medical processes—and a new specialty was born.

Having had such a positive experience with hypnosis for their fertility issues, many of these clients then continued on with me for pregnancy and birth support, and, in some cases, for lactation assistance. The positive pregnancy test result is often just the beginning, especially for those who have had a miscarriage(s) or complications. The first trimester can be stressful, and hypnosis can help make the journey through it, and every other milestone along the way, more peaceful. I call my babies (well, I call them "my" babies, first of all — can I say "lol" with a little winky emoji here?) little-round-heads because babies conceived/born with hypnosis don't tend to have the "pointy" or "cone" shape to their heads that can occur during more stressful birth experiences. They also tend to be very relaxed or "chill."

HF in no way conflicts with conventional or complementary and alternative medicine. I work with women and/or couples to assist them in conceiving naturally, or as an adjunct to Assisted Reproductive Technology (ART). Hypnosis supports whatever direction you have elected to pursue, and helps you get the most out of the process. The focus is not my concern; my goal is to help you to realize your dream: a healthy baby.

Chapter 2

POSITIVE WORDS CREATE POSITIVE OUTCOMES

"Do not anticipate trouble or worry about what may never happen. Keep in the sunlight."
— Benjamin Franklin

Let's start with *infertility*. This word itself is anti-hypnotic (negative) and therefore we will instead refer to *fertility* here. The subconscious mind is literal. You are the sum total of all that you repeat to yourself in the privacy of your own mind — it is essential that you choose your thoughts carefully. Compounding suggestion and repetition are methods of affecting the subconscious mind. If you choose to think *infertile* rather than fertile, you are literally reinforcing a hypnotic suggestion. The subconscious mind responds to emotion — what sort of emotion does the word infertile dredge up for you?

The word infertile is an example of what we in the industry call *painted* or *charged words*. Words like *infertile, donor eggs, old eggs,* and the like elicit sharp images in the mind, and/or a visceral response, which in turn reinforce fears or blocks at the subconscious level, further exacerbating the issue. Understanding what hypnotic suggestion is and where it comes from, how the subconscious mind works, and how to utilize hypnotic effect to your benefit can help you create positive environments in your own life.

The subconscious mind is goal-achieving. It's designed to help you get what you want. However, it is non-thinking, so it does not consider whether what it has determined you want is actually what you want. If you are looking at getting a new car, let's say a brand-new purple Dodge Challenger, your subconscious mind will start finding purple Dodge Challengers for you, and you will see them everywhere. The same happens with infertility. If you are focused on being infertile, your subconscious mind will help you to achieve it. It will find stories, reasons, possible medical problems, negative statistics... virtually anything in line with what it perceives to be your goal: infertility.

The subconscious mind is the realm of habit. You could actually use the words interchangeably. How do we create a habit? By repetition. How do we impact the subconscious mind? Repetition. We go to the gym regularly, and it becomes a habit. We drink a bottle and a half of wine every Saturday night, and it becomes a habit. We smoke a pack of cigarettes a day—we don't have to think about it, we just do it. It's a habit. We are in the habit of stopping by the store to pick up a carton; we have a habit of lighting a cigarette when we start the car. If we are having coffee, we light up a cigarette. There is no need for conscious involvement—smoking is a habit. The subconscious mind smokes for us. We may find ourselves outside smoking a cigarette when we need a break at work—sometimes before we have realized that we are in need of a break, and sometimes not knowing quite how we got out there.

A habit is something you don't have to think about. It has been ingrained in the subconscious mind, and the subconscious mind executes it for you... flawlessly. The subconscious mind doesn't distinguish between good and bad. A habit is neither good nor bad—it is just something you do without thinking about it. Most of us consider smoking to be a bad habit. We think of going to the gym regularly as a good habit. We speak in terms of study habits—though whether we are always organized and have a study system, or don't study at all and just cram the night before an exam, both are habits. One good, one bad? Maybe. That, as Einstein would say, is all relative. Organization and planning might seem to be the obvious choice for a good habit, but many people do exceptionally well on exams they didn't study for until the last minute. The point is that no matter how they are labeled, each of these examples is a habit.

This little poem is a favorite of mine; it says it all:

I am your constant companion. I am your greatest helper or heaviest burden. I will push you onward or drag you down to failure. I am completely at your command. Half the things you do you might just as well turn over to me—and I will be able to do them quickly and correctly.

I am easily managed—you must merely be firm with me. Show me exactly how you want something done, and after a few lessons I will do it automatically. I am the servant of all great people; and, alas, of all failures as well. Those who are great, I have made great. Those who are failures, I have made failures.

I am not a machine, though I work with all the precision of a machine plus the intelligence of a human being. You may run me for profit or turn me for ruin—it makes no difference to me.

Take me, train me, be firm with me, and I will place the world at your feet. Be easy with me and I will destroy you.

Who Am I? **I Am Habit**.

—*Anonymous*

There is also a tendency for the subconscious mind to miss the true meaning of any given statement because of something called, in the world of hypnosis, pharsing. Pharsing occurs with words that have a *not* derivative such as don't or can't. *I can't find my car keys* often results in being unable to find the car keys even though they are right in front of you, or they are in a place you have looked several times and someone else just picks them up and says, *"these car keys?"* to your chagrin. So, in thinking of the word infertile we have the charged issue; in thinking *I'm not infertile* we have the pharsing issue: *I'm* not *infertile* = *I'm infertile*.

There are many definitions of hypnosis. We hear terms such as relaxation, suggestibility, and hypnotizability. We may think in terms of clinical hypnosis, psychology, private practice. The most clear and concise definition of hypnosis I can give you is this: hypnosis is the bypass of the critical faculty (more about this in chapter 3) of the mind allowing access to the subconscious.

Using different types of hypnotic induction methods, a certified hypnotherapist in an office setting will guide you into the hypnotic state. Progressive relaxation (relaxing different parts of the body in succession) and guided imagery are probably the most familiar methods; however, there are many ways to induce hypnosis, and it is important to note that one does not have to be relaxed for hypnosis to occur. The goal is to access the subconscious mind. After all, if it were possible to simply create the necessary change consciously there would be no fertility issues to speak of, and no need for hypnosis to enhance fertility.

Each and every person who wishes to be hypnotized can be hypnotized under the right conditions. It is a fallacy that strong-minded people cannot be hypnotized. In fact, strong-minded people often have some of the greatest success because when they decide to do something, they do it. There are three requirements necessary for hypnosis to occur: a minimal level of intelligence, an ability to follow simple instructions, and a willingness to be hypnotized. (Of course, you do need someone skilled in the practice to hypnotize you.) No hypnotist can make you do anything against your will; no one can control your mind. I am known to joke with people that if we could do such things, the world would be run by power-crazed hypnotists who would hardly need to maintain private practices working with smoking cessation, weight loss, and fertility issues.

Being hypnotized is a learned skill. Some are better at it initially, but anyone can improve with practice. The mind does not have to be quiet or still during the hypnotic process, which makes hypnosis preferable to meditation for some people. Hypnosis is a participatory process. The hypnotherapist works with you during your session to create the most powerful session for you based on the information you provide, and the goals you desire to achieve.

It is sometimes said that all hypnosis is self-hypnosis. What this means is that hypnosis is not done *to* you — it is a natural state that we access daily. There are some issues for which simple self-hypnosis will be sufficient, and others that require the facilitation of a professional hypnotherapist. A certified hypnotherapist can help you to accomplish more in just a few sessions than many people can in an entire lifetime.

There are a few misconceptions about hypnosis which I will address here so that you can understand and benefit from the process:

> *I might get stuck in hypnosis.* This will not happen. Even if the hypnotherapist were to leave the building and forget about you completely, you would do one of two things: drift into a natural sleep for a few minutes or simply open your eyes.

> *My secrets will be revealed!* Hypnosis is not a truth serum. You are always aware of

the process and in control of what is said or not said at any time during the session.

I don't want anyone to control my mind! Therapeutic hypnosis is a state of heightened awareness, a tool with which you can tap into the power of your own mind and create positive changes in your life. The protective critical faculty of the mind ensures that your morals, values, and beliefs are kept intact.

I don't think I can be hypnotized! What if I can't go under? "Go under" is a poor choice of words to describe the hypnotic state. It is the stuff of movies. During hypnosis you are not asleep or unconscious and, in fact, you experience a state of heightened awareness. Relaxation complements hypnosis nicely but is not a requirement. Hypnosis can occur when standing, sitting and relaxing, with eyes open or closed. There simply needs to be a willingness on your part to participate. By following the instructions of the hypnotherapist, you will be able to benefit from hypnosis.

What if I fall asleep? It makes no difference whether you "remain awake" or "fall asleep" during a hypnosis session. This is only the opinion of your conscious mind which really has no way to gauge the hypnotic state and therefore may *think* you have fallen asleep when you are simply benefiting from a pleasant state. And even if you were to fall asleep, the subconscious mind does not. It always hears, it always pays attention.

Will you make me cluck like a chicken? To this I will smilingly respond, "Only if you think it is therapeutically necessary..." It is a myth that people can be made to do things against their will; you will not do something during the hypnotic state that you would not do otherwise. Hypnosis simply affords you access to the more powerful part of your mind—the subconscious mind—where you can make changes that will benefit you. You are always in control.

My mind is too sharp to be hypnotized. Only weak-minded individuals can be hypnotized. This is just not so. A sharp mind is an asset in accessing and benefiting from the state of hypnosis. Different induction methods will benefit different learning styles or information processing abilities. A skilled hypnotherapist will utilize your individual style and intelligence level to facilitate the very best experience for you. Hypnosis is a participatory process. The professional hypnotherapist functions, in a sense, as a guide. Self-hypnosis, like meditation, is a highly effective method for reducing stress and creating an inner calm. A hypnotherapist trained in HypnoFertility® is necessary to facilitate some of the deeper work outlined in this book, but there is much you can do yourself. Hypnosis (used interchangeably with the word trance by some) can be described as concentrated and directed daydreaming. Whereas the word sleep is sometimes used to describe the trance state, you are not asleep while in hypnosis. A person in hypnosis is aware of his/her surroundings in a detached sort of way and is simply more receptive to acceptable suggestions.

Can everyone be hypnotized? Yes. *Can I prevent it?* Yes, provided you know it is happening. Therapeutically, you just don't follow the instructions. With the waking hypnosis that occurs through repetition like in advertising, you just have to pay attention so that nothing can sneak in. The *Cancel Technique* (see chapter 4) is your best friend in this case.

Can a hypnotist make you do something against your will? No. But, again, advertising convinces us that something is for our own good, that we must have a certain something, that there is truth in a particular statement. Advertisers trigger our emotions and tap into our hopes, fears, and dreams to sell us cars, attract us to restaurants, influence our vote. Many media messages convince us we cannot have a baby. This is also hypnosis — these are also hypnotic suggestions. This book will teach you how to protect yourself from the media, advertisers, naysayers, inconsiderate medical personnel; in short, to *de*hypnotize yourself and take back control of your life.

Chapter 3

HYPNOSIS HELPS YOU USE
YOUR WHOLE BRAIN

"Any idea, plan, or purpose may be placed in the mind through repetition of thought."
— Napoleon Hill

To understand hypnosis, you need to be aware of how the conscious and subconscious minds function. Imagine that the human brain is divided into two main sections: the left hemisphere, associated with the conscious mind, which is logical, linear, analytical, rational, decision-making; and the right hemisphere, associated with the subconscious mind, which is intuitive, imaginative, emotional, non-thinking, goal-achieving, protective, irrational. I always joke that the conscious mind is the part that reads all the self-help books and watches *Oprah*! It knows what we need to do, and even how to do it. However, the conscious mind is the weaker part of the mind, and when the two are in conflict it will lose to subconscious programming if we don't address that also.

The left-brained view of the world is considered to be the scientific perspective, regardless of the fact that we cannot create anything with our left brains that we have not first imagined with our right. In the words of the world-renowned genius Albert Einstein: "Imagination is more important than knowledge. For knowledge is limited, whereas imagination embraces the entire world, stimulating progress, giving birth to evolution." Thinking outside the box is an ability we need to develop if we desire to transcend the limits of so-called reality and create success.

The subconscious mind—the more powerful part of your mind—responds to imagery, patterns, poetry, music, metaphor. The critical faculty of the mind basically functions as a door or screen, a sort of psychological filter, that protects information that is in (or is trying to enter) the subconscious mind, whether it is positive or negative. To create change at the subconscious level, one must bypass the critical faculty. The most effective method to achieve this is hypnosis.

Any form of startle or shock will instantly bypass the critical faculty of the mind. Formal hypnotic induction by a certified hypnotherapist is designed to distract the conscious mind (bypass the critical faculty), whereby bringing the subconscious to the forefront. During the hypnotic state there is a physiological change in the brain which basically balances its two hemispheres and strengthens communication pathways between them. This establishes receptivity to suggestions for change in the form of imagery, pictures, patterns, and emotion which the hypnotherapist creates based on information provided by you during your intake session. I've found that a lot of the work I do in my office is more of what I term a *de*hypnotizing process. This is because the critical faculty is often bypassed during daily life, leaving your subconscious mind open to suggestions that you are not even aware of. This can be the cause of formidable subconscious blocks.

Fear is an excellent example of what I am talking about. When we are afraid, we revert to our inherent programming. When the fight or flight response (see chapter 5) is triggered, critical thinking is bypassed and our instincts (unconscious) kick in. This is particularly discouraging for fertility because, number one, the reproductive system is not considered necessary for survival and therefore is one of the first systems of the body to be neglected in favor of those necessary to run or fight. Number two, an experience or comment that shocks or startles us will immediately bypass the critical faculty (waking hypnosis) and a follow-up direct suggestion (such as *you will never be able to get pregnant*) is then accepted by the subconscious mind. This is especially true if the suggestion is delivered by someone perceived to be in authority (such as a doctor or nurse) and/or with enough emotion, imagery, color (e.g. television) to create an imprint.

The latest hype in the media is the rising number of infertile couples; it is that infertility is an epidemic. We hear news reports, read articles, hear celebrity gossip, see commercials, watch television shows that continually reinforce the *fact* that it is becoming more and more difficult to conceive. (More hypnotic suggestions.) Reality shows and sitcoms focus on the anguish of infertility, making jokes about the obsessive behaviors often associated with it. Since many women wait until their mid-to-late-thirties, and well into their forties and fifties these days, before starting a family, there is a lot more time for them to receive negative pregnancy input which contributes to negative reinforcement.

At one time pregnancy was a natural experience. People worried about getting pregnant, not about whether or not they could. In the past if a couple didn't conceive right away it was just assumed that it would happen eventually. But these days women are rushing to infertility specialists if they don't conceive on the first "try," and the pressure is extreme. Not to say that there may not be something physically wrong, in which case medical technology is appreciated, but we should not jump to conclusions.

Just as with birthing, we need to consider some type of balance. It's wonderful that medical technology has advanced to where babies and/or mothers are able to survive in cases where they wouldn't have before, but overuse of invasive medical procedures indiscriminately has detracted from birth as a natural experience and turned it into crisis. Our bodies know how to procreate, and they know how to give birth. I believe this is why hypnosis has been so successful with fertility assistance — it facilitates the mind/body/spirit balance which is simply in harmony with nature.

If a woman is 35 years of age or more, she is instantly labeled *high risk* in the medical world. High risk is another example of the painted words we discussed earlier. Their effects can be devastating. Because the language of the subconscious mind is emotion, any words which elicit emotion will cause a powerful impact. When a medical expert tells you that you are high risk it triggers a fear response which automatically bypasses your critical faculty, driving in the suggestion. Subsequent suggestions then have direct access to the subconscious as the critical mind is actively wrestling with the shock triggered by the initial diagnosis.

If a woman is not yet pregnant but confides in her physician that she is currently contemplating becoming pregnant, an insensitive comment (intentional or otherwise) can have a distressing effect. The subconscious mind is protective, yet it is non-thinking. Should the literal subconscious interpret *high risk* to be too dangerous, it can instantly put up a roadblock to pregnancy. Fortunately, hypnosis can quickly, and usually quite easily, reverse such an effect.

Chapter 4

YOU CAN STOP NEGATIVE THOUGHTS

*"Remember, no one can make you feel
inferior without your consent."*
— Eleanor Roosevelt

In chapter 2, I discussed the impact of words on the subconscious, such as with advertising. There are even sales and marketing books that teach you ways to access the subconscious mind. Depending on your purpose you might find this intriguing. The important thing is to know that you are not at the mercy of these experiences. You can protect yourself with a simple cognitive behavioral therapy (CBT) thought-stopping technique.

Becoming more mindful of your thoughts will make it easier for you to choose your state of mind. Upon hearing a negative thought or suggestion, say emphatically to yourself *STOP* or *CANCEL* and imagine drawing a big, red "X" through the thought in your mind. Or, if you prefer, you can imagine an eraser, or the delete key of a computer. I call this the cancel technique. The point is to use emotion and imagery to communicate with the subconscious.

One of my clients uses the three red x's (XXX) and the buzzer sound from the gameshow *Family Feud*. I use the cancel technique whenever I go to a doctor and they want my medical history. I cancel out any suggestions of cancer, heart disease, diabetes, high blood pressure, etc. that are projected onto me through discussion of parents, grandparents, and the rest of my family tree. After all, if I have to accept predisposition to everything every person in my family has had, I may as well lie down in my coffin right now. Personally, I prefer to cancel those suggestions and focus on good health.

I have taught the cancel technique to thousands of people through seminars, classes, and even in private session. It's an awesome tool that is a simple yet powerful way to redirect your thoughts. *As you think so shall you be*. This universal law is quoted in various forms by world renowned speakers Dr. Wayne Dyer and Deepak Chopra. Both reference versions of this exact thought stopping process, and Dr. Dyer has gone to great lengths in numerous publications to expound on these principles.

Chapter 5

THE POWER OF THE MIND

"For one who has controlled the mind, it is the best of friends, but for one who has failed to do so, it remains the greatest enemy."
— The Bhagavad Gita

Many women are experiencing infertility due to physiological issues. Hypnosis can help with these issues in many ways including stress reduction and direct application complementary to medical procedures. Subconscious blocks have been shown to cause infertility whether there is a physiological problem or not. Unresolved sexual trauma, abortion (self or others), miscarriage, abusive relationships, fear of imitating someone else's parenting mistakes, and sudden death or injury to a loved one are only a few examples of the subconscious blocks I've encountered that were interfering with conception. The key is to remember that you may not have any idea that these or other experiences have so profoundly affected you.

I have dealt specifically with clients' blocks created by having comforted a friend through a teenage abortion experience; having had a brief, but frightening, early childhood encounter with a seriously disabled individual; the grisly story of a grandmother's (*"my father's mother's"*) murder during the holocaust; the trauma of attending what turned out to be the stillbirth of a younger sibling; watching an episode about the death of a baby on the 1970s television show *Little House on the Prairie*; being the punching bag of a messed up 18-year-old mother; being held at gunpoint by an abusive husband; having endured brutalization of pets as punishment for some minor transgression; having been terrorized at the age of 10 by a film about childbirth that featured a lot of blood and screaming; having been held hostage during a school shooting and being afraid that getting pregnant might somehow result in becoming the parent of a murderer; the list goes on.

Some of these things may seem appropriate causes of subconscious blocks. Some may not. But, as I've said before, the subconscious mind is not about logic—it is about emotion. And perception. And interpretation. This is what the unbridled power of the mind can do. And this is why we sometimes need some help to deal with it.

By the time I see clients for hypnotherapy they have usually already seen a physician, and many have received the diagnosis of unexplained infertility. Quite a few are being treated with acupuncture, and, as you are probably aware, acupuncture is a widely accepted complementary and alternative therapy (CAM) for the treatment of infertility. Reproductive endocrinologists (REs) will sometimes refer their patients to an acupuncturist to complement the in vitro fertilization (IVF) process. Hypnosis, in addition to its positive effects on ART, is a powerful adjunct to acupuncture. The combination of hypnosis and acupuncture can effectively accelerate the fertility process—both natural and medically assisted.

The physiological support that hypnosis provides in relation to ART also enhances acupuncture. Both facilitate healing effects within the nervous system, but in different ways, and for different reasons. Mental/emotional blocks can definitely diminish the benefits of acupuncture, or any treatment. Fortunately, hypnosis can help to release them. If you feel like you are doing (or have done) everything you possibly can and are still not getting pregnant—especially where unexplained infertility is concerned—you may indeed want to look into hypnosis.

Occasionally, women express concern about getting their hopes up. This again plays into the fear and negative thinking I mentioned earlier. It is possible that you will never conceive a baby, but it is also possible that you will. It is important at this stage to release negative thinking—fear of getting your hopes up is negative thinking. Each and every person on the planet is able to deal with disappointment, devastation, disaster… if they have to. But at this point you don't know that you have to.

The subconscious mind does not distinguish between fact and fantasy; therefore, it processes negative thinking about not becoming pregnant as effectively as actually not becoming pregnant. As with anything we want to manifest, it is essential to put our energies all in. If we are only half in because we are trying to avoid disappointment, we might as well be all out. Don't, as the saying goes, borrow trouble. We don't know what the future holds. All that matters is this very moment, and once you've achieved balance of mind/body/spirit you will find you have a new perspective altogether.

I work with women one-on-one and/or with their partners. I also work with male fertility issues. I have sometimes found men to have subconscious blocks similar to those that women experience. I find it interesting that many men, who at the initial infertility medical workup tested normal, are found to have a low sperm count upon retesting a year later. In other words, the emotional strain and stress a couple endures during a year of infertility testing and medical treatment appears to have serious impact on the ability to conceive.

We may forget, or it may never even occur to us, that men can also have unresolved issues involving previous pregnancies or abortions. There are many scenarios which may have caused a man's subconscious mind to put up a protective block, and this can also interfere with conception. Perhaps he's been devastated by a previous partner having had an abortion when he really wanted the child. He may be concerned with repeating abusive behavior stemming from his own childhood experience. In one case, a man had been so traumatized by his first wife having died from a ruthless cancer discovered during what they'd thought was basic fertility treatment, that—despite his _thinking_ that he had moved on and was ready to start a family with his new wife—his subconscious mind would not allow it. In these and other such cases, hypnotic resolution can effectively address the issue and positively effect conception.

Hypnotic patter, not unlike musical lyrics, affects some of the more primitive parts of the brain. Bypassing the critical faculty in this manner, which is necessary to access the emotional, imaginative subconscious mind, is how a CHFT assists with the release of subconscious blocks. Evocation of emotion is the means by which we communicate with the subconscious; it provides an effective method of bypassing the rational, analytical part of the mind. Although both sides of the brain are necessary to correctly interpret spoken words, access to the non-verbal right hemisphere is essential for successful hypnotic process. Though right brain language, such as metaphors, similes, juxtapositions, emotion, poetic device, and hypnotic suggestion may be considered nonsense by the left brain, the impact it has on the subconscious mind is impressive.

Because the subconscious mind responds to metaphor, subconscious purge techniques (see chapter 6) using images like ripping pages out of a book, erasing a blackboard, and erasing and/or editing video clips may be enough to eliminate subconscious blocks. Sometimes, however, we need a stronger tactic. In these cases, we use what is called a hypnotic regression (see chapter 7). An experienced hypnotherapist will be able to evaluate your specific case and determine the course of action that is right for you.

Chapter 6

SUBCONSCIOUS BLOCKS

"With our thoughts we make the world."
— Buddha

Hypnosis is the go-to modality when people need assistance in remembering something, and when they feel they have subconscious blocks. Both my husband, who has been in general hypnotherapy practice for more than 25 years, and I receive referrals from therapists of a more conventional style, that practice forms of talk therapy, analysis, or behavioral modification therapies. I am a big proponent of therapy—the key to growth is in knowing ourselves. Therapy provides opportunity for exploration and understanding that we would be unlikely to find elsewhere. However, when progress is slowed or stalled, straight up therapy may need a boost.

Usually when a person ceases to progress in therapy it is because of a subconscious block. As well as being emotional and goal-achieving, the subconscious mind is also protective.

As I explained earlier, the subconscious mind is non-thinking, non-linear; its language is emotion. The subconscious mind is also protective, and that protective mechanism tends to be the number one contributor to (or cause of) subconscious blocks. Let's take a person who is seriously overweight, for example. We frequently hear that sexual abuse is the cause of people being overweight or obese. Let me be clear, just because someone is overweight does not mean they have sexual abuse issues — there are many reasons people carry extra weight, and it is not accurate to stereotype anyone. But, for our purposes here, this is a great example of how the protective mechanism of the subconscious mind works.

When children are being abused or harmed in any way, they just want it to stop. To be bullied, threatened, molested, screamed at, punched and kicked, shaken — or even worse — is terrifying. Children are extremely vulnerable in that they are little, and they have to rely on adults who may very well be the ones perpetrating the abuse. (This also goes for a woman or a smaller person who is raped or battered by any person of violence.) Fear is one of the strongest (if not *the* strongest) emotions we have. In order to survive, the subconscious mind develops coping mechanisms. One such coping mechanism is overeating.

In the aftermath of an abusive episode a child may wish to be bigger. *If I was bigger this wouldn't happen.* The subconscious mind is literal as well as protective. It will use whatever is at hand to protect us from danger, whether or not the mechanism of choice is in our best interest overall. What the subconscious mind perceives to be bigger, and what a child means in wanting to be big enough to prevent the abuse, are two different things. To be an adult, or a large man, or a police officer is along the lines of what the child is wishing. But that could take a while, if it's possible at all. What is quicker and more convenient is food. Technically, gaining weight is to be bigger. The problem is that the subconscious mind can't take into account the myriad other problems that being overweight can cause: diabetes, high blood pressure, back problems, joint problems, low self-esteem... So, the "cure" does not really help the cause.

It is the same with fertility. I have seen a lot of cases where the subconscious has blocked fertility for reasons less than logical (the subconscious mind is not logical, of course). Many doctors, nurses, speech therapists, occupational therapists, teachers, and any profession that deals with child trauma have subconscious blocks preventing pregnancy. This is because these professionals have seen, or have been trained to handle, the worst possible scenario. They have a powerful emotional imprint of the very worst that could happen (I won't delve into the specifics; you get the idea, no need for painted words), so as far as the subconscious mind is concerned: *if we don't get pregnant, none of this can happen to us.* Done deal. As with the weight example, not getting pregnant may prevent a person from personally experiencing something they would never want to, but it causes other problems if you do not wish to be childless. Low self-esteem, anxiety, depression, self-deprecation, insomnia; damage to relationships, marital strain, feelings of isolation; emotional and financial devastation. Just for starters.

As I mentioned in chapter 5, the same is true for those who have had traumatic personal experiences such as having had an abortion or miscarriage, having to be responsible for a handicapped sibling, having constantly heard terrible birth stories from their mothers or other significant women in their lives, nearly dying at birth themselves, having abusive parents and not wanting to repeat the cycle of violence. Fear-based issues too numerous to mention here can elicit the same protective response from the subconscious mind: *if we don't get pregnant, we have no problem.* Except, of course, we do.

Hypnosis is the key to unlocking the subconscious. Potential blocks reside in the subconscious mind; therefore, we must access the subconscious mind to remove them. A subconscious purge technique, which is basically a cleansing or releasing of subconscious fears, is typically enough to eliminate obstructions to pregnancy — we don't even need to know what the block is or might have been. Sometimes we find out, sometimes not; but none of that matters once the path to healthy pregnancy and birth has been cleared.

A subconscious purge may be done interactively, where you and your hypnotherapist speak back and forth to one another. It also may be done silently, where the hypnotherapist guides, but the process occurs in the privacy of your own mind. Depending upon the facilitator, and the circumstances, nonverbal signals such as raising a finger or nodding the head may be used to navigate the process. If it is determined that a block still remains following a subconscious purge, a hypnotic regression will likely be necessary.

Chapter 7

REGRESSION TO CAUSE

"Who controls the past controls the future: who controls the present controls the past."
— *George Orwell*

As I mentioned in the previous chapter, a subconscious purge is generally enough to address pregnancy obstacles. I find the subconscious purge to be effective in about 90 percent of cases, but sometimes hypnotic regression, or what we in the field call *regression to cause*, is needed to overcome a deep-seated problem. There are various regression methods, though I find building an affect bridge (emotional connection), based on your most evident feelings, to be most effective. The affect bridge engages the subconscious mind more effectively (emotion being the language of the subconscious mind) than any other method, and it appeals less to the conscious mind (which sometimes interferes or tries too hard to "help" with the process). The ultimate goal is for you to travel back in time, within the subconscious mind, to the incident, event, or situation that initiated the block.

For example, some women say that they feel frustrated about their fertility issues. Others may be sad, angry, impatient, apathetic, enraged, etc. Each person's experience is unique, and I have no expectations as to which feelings someone should have. Once I've determined the focus of the regression, I will typically use a rapid induction (which produces the necessary level of hypnosis in less than three minutes) method, and then guide you back through whatever feelings come up until we reach the initial sensitizing event (ISE). This is the first time you experienced the feeling(s) that produced the presenting symptoms (SPE).

My purpose with regression is to find whatever it is that initially caused the subconscious mind to impose a protective mechanism that eventually resulted in fertility issues. The symptom producing event (SPE), perhaps an unexplained infertility diagnosis, or a medical diagnosis such as low AMH/high FSH, endometriosis, or some other type of physiological condition, is what typically lands a person in my office. In the search for the ISE we will most likely encounter several subsequent sensitizing events (SSE) which are the various experiences we have throughout our lives that reinforce the subconscious mind's original reaction to the initial incident. We don't know how or why a subconscious block has been created until we have completed the uncovering process and arrived at the ISE. The initial sensitizing event may not seem to be consciously related to the subsequent sensitizing events; however, due to trance logic (the function of the non-thinking subconscious mind), I deal with what emerges in the session and make no judgments.

Because suggestion is strengthened by repetition or compounding, there is actually a chain of events that ultimately leads to the fertility issue. The initial event almost always occurs before the age of three and is not usually consciously recognized. If someone comes in and says, "I want a regression, I had a teacher in the seventh grade whose baby died and now I have a block...," that is most likely not the initial event, no matter how certain this person may be that it is. I will keep that information in mind, and I will make sure not to have expectations either way as I facilitate the regression.

> - ISE - Initial Sensitizing Event
> - SSE - Subsequent Sensitizing Event
> - SPE - Symptom Producing Event
> - SIE - Symptom Intensifying Event

Creating an affect bridge, finding a key emotion that helps someone return to important moments in the past, is one of the hypnotherapist's most important strategies. An example of a fertility-focused affect bridge follows:

Please note that the purpose of this book is to assist persons experiencing fertility difficulties to understand how hypnotherapy can help. Any examples or referenced protocols included here are for informational purposes only, and not intended for self-hypnosis practice. Nor is this an instruction manual for hypnotherapists.

Client: I am devastated that I cannot have a baby. I feel that my life is incomplete. My husband is wonderful, but I can hardly stand to look at him. I feel like such a failure.

During the initial intake the HypnoFertility® Therapist (HFT) determines what feelings are most evident. She then initiates hypnosis and builds the affect bridge.

Moving back in time:

Client: I'm outside. I'm in the park, playing tag with my friends.

HFT: How does it feel to be outside, playing tag with your friends?

C: Wonderful! I'm so strong and I have so much energy.

HFT anchors these positive feelings to the breath so that they may be easily accessed later.

Client connects with her feelings in a pleasant situation which helps in creating the affect bridge.

Moving back again:

C: I'm just little, I'm riding a big horsey, his name is Santana…

HFT reinforces the positive connection of this second experience, and then moves on utilizing the presenting feelings (i.e. devastation and failure) of the symptom producing event (SPE) to guide the client further back.

C: Indoors. I'm at the doctor's. He just told me I can't get pregnant. [Begins to cry.]

HFT: How does that make you feel?

C: I'm crushed, devastated. I feel like the bottom has dropped out of my stomach.

HFT: Are these feelings of being crushed, devastated, bottom dropping out of your stomach new to you or familiar?

Familiar feelings indicate we have not uncovered the ISE and must continue on. If the client responds with "new" we will then look at reframing the event. We will not do the transformational piece, or reframe the event, until we have reached the ISE.

C: Familiar.

HFT continues constructing the affect bridge with the emotional and visceral feelings of being crushed, devastated, the bottom dropping out of the stomach.

C: I'm lying in bed with my boyfriend. He just broke up with me. He knew he was going to do it, but he slept with me anyway.

HFT: How does that make you feel?

C: I'm devastated. I feel sick to my stomach. It's like my world is coming undone. I can't believe it, I thought we were so happy. [Sobbing]

HFT determines client's age during this event.

C: Twenty. I'm in college. He was my first real love. I thought he was. We were going to get married, have a family, and now it's just over, just like that, so cruel.

HFT establishes the newness or familiarity of the sensations of devastation, sick to stomach...

C: Familiar.

HFT asks if client has made a decision at this time.

C: You can't trust anyone, can't let anyone close to you.

HFT continues on with these familiar feelings.

C: I'm sitting on the ground. I'm crying. I fell off the monkey bars in the school yard. No, I was pushed off. That mean kid, Billy Brown, pushed me off. He's such a bully, he's always hurting somebody. He pushed me.

HFT: You're on the ground crying, he pushed you off the monkey bars, how does that make you feel?

C: I'm mad and sad. My tummy hurts too.

As the client regresses in age it may become apparent in her choice of vocabulary, and the childlike sound of her voice. However, people maintain the ability to converse in adult terms as well.

HFT: Are these feelings new to you or familiar?

C: Familiar.

Once again, the HFT moves the client through time toward the initial sensitizing event. Note that we are concerned with the feelings rather than the specific event. It is possible, and even probable, that as we continue back in time the events accessed will seem less and less directly connected to the issue. Remember, the subconscious mind does not adhere to the logic of the conscious mind.

C: (I'm) inside. It's quiet. Dark.

HFT: Alone or with people?

C: Alone, but I sense a presence.

Quiet, dark, alone but sensing a presence are clues that the client may be in utero.

HFT: What are you aware of?

C: Loss. A devastating loss. I feel sobbing.

HFT: Tell me about the sobbing.

C: I feel it but it's not me. I'm not sobbing but I feel it in my being. I feel like I am a part of this sobbing.

HFT: How does that make you feel?

C: Devastated. It's haunting. My stomach hurts, it feels like the bottom has dropped out of it.

HFT: Are these feelings new or familiar?

C: New. They're new. I haven't felt anything like this before. It's terrible. I want to make it stop.

HFT has reached the original event, that is, the ISE. She will need a little more information before proceeding to the transformational piece.

HFT: How can you make it stop?

C: I don't know.

HFT informs the client that while in the hypnotic state she has access to a lot of interesting tools, and that she can use them (simply by intention) to get more information if she needs it. Pause…

HFT: What's happening?

C: I can hear better now. I'm inside my mom. It's my mom sobbing. My dad hit her, he hurt her real bad. She's scared. She doesn't know what to do. It's not safe. It's not safe to be pregnant. He could hurt the baby. She should have been more careful. She's blaming herself, but she didn't know he would do this.

HFT: What can you do to make this better?

It is time to resolve and reframe the experience. Sometimes the incident will resolve itself with the client's realization and/or verbalization of what occurred. Other possible resolution techniques include having the client consult with her adult self (who contributes adult knowledge, wisdom, and experience to the situation), dialoguing techniques (where the client has a discussion with an essential element of the experience such as an aborted fetus, an abusive parent, or even God), client reframes the incident by creating a new and better outcome, etc. The subconscious mind cannot distinguish between reality and imagination, therefore the transformational hypnotherapy piece, which changes the effect of the experience at the subconscious level, is extremely powerful in the completion of releasing subconscious blocks. The client may have an idea about ways to "rewrite" the scene or the HFT may make some suggestions.

C: Adult me comes into the room and comforts Mom. She (client's adult self) tells mom that everything is okay, and that help is available. She calls the police and they arrest my dad and put him in jail. Mom feels better and now she knows it is safe to be pregnant because she's not alone.

HFT: What do you know about it being safe to be pregnant?

C: I know it's safe too! It's okay because I have the resources to have a healthy pregnancy.

HFT asks whether the client has anything else to take care of at this time.

C: No, it's okay now.

HFT guides the client back to present time, stopping at each SSE on the way back, and reframing along the way. Many times, the SSEs are already adjusted in the subconscious based on the reframe of the ISE.

C: Billy tried to push me off the monkey bars, but I knew he was going to try it and I was too smart for him. He fell down trying to push me and he's crying. Now the principal is coming and taking Billy into the school. The principal knows what he was up to and he's gonna get in trouble.

HFT: But you're okay?

C: I'm okay, because I trusted myself and I was careful.

HFT: Anything else you need to do here?

C: Nope.

HFT resumes forward movement.

C: I just broke up with my boyfriend.

HFT: How do you feel?

C: Great. I've known for a while that he's not what he seems to be, and I certainly don't want to spend my life with him.

HFT: What happens next?

C: I just told him it wasn't meant to be.

HFT: How does that make you feel?

C: Glad that I didn't waste my time with him. I'm proud of myself.

HFT: Anything else you need to do here?

C: No, it's good.

Client arrives at the SPE.

C: I'm at the doctor's office. He just told me that my pregnancy test result is positive! I'm going to have a baby! My husband is so happy! We're both just thrilled!

I don't direct the reframe nor do I critique or judge it. In this case the client chooses not to receive the infertility diagnosis at all, and instead receive positive pregnancy test results. She could have chosen many different ways to reframe; she knows which one is right for her.

HFT: How do you feel?

C: Amazing! I knew I could do it; I knew I could have a baby.

HFT progresses the client into the future which she envisions to include all that she desires to create. (You must be able to imagine something in order to create it in the physical world.)

In the above case it is apparent that not all reinforcing events, or SSEs, are logically connected to the infertility diagnosis. However, the feeling connection is quite clear. The feelings caused by the physical and emotional trauma that happened to her mother while the client was in utero are then reinforced when she is pushed off monkey bars in the school yard by a bully. These feelings are again compounded when she is dumped by an insensitive boyfriend, which results in her decision to not trust anyone. Though seemingly unrelated, the protective subconscious mind has responded by blocking conception, resulting in the infertility diagnosis.

Examples of other such seemingly unrelated subconscious ISE/SSE chains are:

- Anxious feelings are created in a premature baby that has to be fed with tubes. These feelings are reinforced during a childhood experience where Mommy has to be away for a couple of weeks, and then compounded by a car accident in early adulthood. The result is a fear of elevators, though no elevator-specific initial or subsequent events occurred.

- A person with a fear of flying (SPE) may have SSEs that include falling off a roof, falling out of a wagon, and an ISE of being born by an emergency cesarean. Again, no flying-related events.

*** *Remember: it is how the subconscious mind originally perceived and interpreted experiences, and subsequently strung them together, that matters.* ***

Chapter 8

THERE IS POWER IN THE PAST

"Fall seven times. Stand up Eight."
— *Japanese proverb*

She sat quietly coloring in her book, soothed by the silence of early morning. She treasured the sense of security suggested by the soft light; and the gift of gentleness she could almost touch. Carefully she applied color to the page, delighting in knowing she could choose what she liked. She could create beauty. She could enjoy peace.

Suddenly there was chaos. She watched detached—almost disinterested—as a little girl's body flew across the room and crashed into the wall above the bed. As though in slow motion, the scene unfolded: the little girl's body as it collapsed onto the neatly made bed; the tiny arm jamming into the space where the mattress met the wall. The blows that followed looked painful, though she was actually more concerned about the little girl's shame, as her clothing tore away beneath the pummeling strikes, exposing areas that should be private, should be respected.

Where that idea came from, she didn't really know. Her ears hurt from all the shrieking and screaming. The little girl made hardly a sound beyond the wind being knocked brutally from her lungs, and an occasional gasp which might have been for air. She didn't usually make much sound until afterward, and then sometimes she hardly had the strength.

Time goes by so fast when you are having fun with a friend, or maybe riding a roller coaster, or playing at the park. But at other times it is painfully slow. Times like this. She worried that someone would hear. She hated the looks they would give her, but before she could ponder this further, she was distracted from her worries by a smell—familiar yet vague. She couldn't tell if she really smelled something, or if it was maybe something triggered by the throbbing in her head or the ringing in her ears. Sometimes that happened. You could think you actually smelled something, but it was really an extension of another sense, or some kind of projection caused perhaps by injury.

If she did in fact smell it, the smell was coppery, kind of faint, or maybe vague would be a better word. She was aware of warmth. She was warm—hot even—feverish. Time was playing tricks again. She heard another sound, closer than the others. Sobbing. Heart-wrenching sobbing. She felt a slight stickiness, kind of out-of-sorts. The light faded, disappeared for a while.

She was thinking again. Berating herself for wearing the little jumper, although it was her favorite. Pants were better, safer. Long pants, or at the very least, a pair of thick tights. At least there was a pretense of protection from the blows. They didn't help much but it was better than shorts or sundresses. She felt weak; drained. She dragged herself off the bed in the fading afternoon light and made her way across the room where she retrieved her coloring book from the floor, and carefully picked up her scattered crayons. She'd better tidy up. She'd better be good.

This type of childhood abuse is all too familiar in the lives of many of my fertility clients. As a hypnotherapist I often bear witness to this type of revisited experience, and it unfolds in much the same manner, the descriptions as vivid as one would actually expect in "reality." Presented from a first-person perspective it provides invaluable insight into the possible subconscious patterns that can develop, including what may seem to be illogical fears of quiet—an underlying sense of constant dread or "calm before the storm." I include the above piece so that you may have compassion and understanding for anyone who has ever lived this experience. Including yourself. It is said that we must release our history in order to move forward. I agree completely. But in order to fully release our history, we first must embrace it.

There is a fine line between having compassion for one's trauma and becoming or remaining the eternal victim. No one enjoys constantly dealing with the victim personality. We all know the type: they preface every encounter with their claim to misery. "I'm a victim of sexual abuse," "I'm the child of an alcoholic," "I had a bad childhood," etc. Wayne Dyer puts it well: "Your biography becomes your biology."

Refusal to let go of the past results in *dis*ease. That's not to say that we can't have compassion for people; in fact, we should. However, there is a fine line between being supportive and being an enabler. When we enable someone, we help keep them stuck in their problems. We can use our awareness of our own past experiences to help ourselves and others if we choose to.

We've all had the experience of picking up the phone and hearing that all-too-familiar voice immediately start in on all that is negative… and we've felt our natural energy drain instantly. Some of us have justified the pattern in ourselves by explaining our need to warn people of our shortcomings so they won't be disappointed in us. Some of us have been raised to think that the ever-sacrificing persona is to be revered — that martyrdom is a desirable practice. Whatever our justification, this is a pattern that must be broken. If we are unwilling to heal these issues, we will be unable to achieve our goals—be they fertility, happiness, abundance, or anything else.

Addressing these issues with hypnosis does not have to be a lengthy and/or messy process. Hypnosis differs greatly from traditional forms of therapy, and clients are often pleasantly surprised at how much they can release in a relatively short amount of time. Hypnosis is considered rapid-change therapy. It is solution-focused and goal-oriented. It dovetails nicely with the self-help or spiritual works you might be familiar with: Wayne Dyer, Louise Hay, Eckhart Tolle, Deepak Chopra, Caroline Myss, Tony Robbins, Dr. Phil, Doreen Virtue, Clarissa Pinkola Estes, and others. In fact, people who have spent years working with some or all of the aforementioned authors and speakers have reported amazing leaps to the next level after just a few sessions of hypnotherapy.

Chapter 9

CHANGE YOUR MIND – CHANGE YOUR LIFE

"Infinite patience produces immediate results."
— A Course in Miracles

Stress is a major culprit in health issues, and fertility is no exception. The best way I can illustrate the effects of stress is as the switch to the autonomic nervous system (ANS) getting stuck in the fight or flight mode. The ANS regulates the functions of our internal organs including the heart, stomach, and intestines. It also controls some of our muscles. There are two branches to the ANS: the sympathetic and the parasympathetic nervous systems (SNS and PNS). The SNS and the PNS are polar opposites. They basically complement each other in a sort of tug-of-war-like fashion, which helps the body to maintain homeostasis (inner-stability).

Fight or flight is a common term for the sympathetic branch of the ANS. The fight or flight response activates instantaneously when we are in any way threatened. This is the body's way of mobilizing energies essential for survival. This is supposed to be a short-term response — we are not designed for prolonged lengths of fight or flight.

When the fight or flight response is activated, the brain revs us up through the release of stressor hormones such as cortisol and adrenaline. These are then directed to the areas considered necessary for self-preservation. It is really quite simple: we need to stand and fight, or we need to run. NOW. The heartbeat increases because we need more blood. The pupils dilate so we can take in more of what is happening. Energy is directed into our limbs because we need them to run or fight. We do not, however, need to be digesting or reproducing in times of such strife. Energy designated for those systems is redirected to the fight or flight zones.

The problem we have as humans these days is that our brains are not effectively wired for contemporary threats. Basically, they haven't caught up with our rapid evolution. At one time we faced immediate dangers. If we encountered a ferocious tiger, we had to fight it, or we had to escape from it. We won, we lost, or we survived to live another day. But it was over. The ANS functions beautifully under these circumstances: immediate threat = sympathetic nervous system triggered, kicks into immediate action. Threat resolved = body restored to balance by the parasympathetic nervous system.

Let's take a moment to imagine a cat. Just an everyday housecat, minding its own business, sitting in the garden. Suddenly the cat sees a vicious dog lunging toward it, and immediately the cat's hackles are up, it is hissing, spitting, and takes off up into a tree. What has happened is the cat's sympathetic nervous system has been triggered — fight or flight response. Immediate danger. The cat doesn't have to think about it, it responds instinctively. As soon as the threat is over the cat saunters down from the tree, sprawls out in the grass, licks its fur, and maybe takes a nap. The parasympathetic nervous system has kicked in, and the cat goes into rejuvenation mode. This is how it is supposed to work.

Unfortunately, the types of threats we face as modern-day humans are constant. Our tigers (or vicious dogs in our housecat's case) are everywhere. They are in the trees, and on the grass, and in our beds (and heads) at night. They lurk, silently, inside our wine cellars; they crouch behind our coffee pots. They are the grumbly lines at Starbucks, and the gridlock on the expressway. Lurking. Always close. Always watching.

The tigers are our e-mail. They are the constant text messages and phone calls. They are the requirement to be so readily available that we have to take the iPhone to the bathroom with us. Our tigers are the barrage of never-ending bills, ever-increasing debt, extended work weeks, demanding bosses, deadlines, ceaseless obligations... We cannot run, and we cannot hide from these tigers. Every day (and sometimes all night) we have to engage. There is always another tiger.

Hence, we end up in the fight or flight mode a <u>LOT</u>, continually doused with stressor hormones. Energy is syphoned from systems not needed for survival—the reproductive system in particular. Hypnosis is the solution to taming these relentless tigers. Hypnosis facilitates a calming of the mind, a soothing of the nervous system. It triggers the parasympathetic (aka feed and breed or rest and digest) branch of the ANS, the natural counter to the sympathetic branch. Because we do face relentless stress, we must learn how to manage our own internal environment. Physiologically, the deep hypnotic state amounts to the exact opposite of the fight or flight response.

In his book *Boundless Energy*, Deepak Chopra discusses the mind/body connection and the body's "internal pharmacy." Dr. Chopra finds the mind/body phenomenon so obvious that he thinks it is amazing that modern medicine has overlooked it to the extent it has. According to Dr. Chopra, neurochemicals and neuropeptides have an essential role in physiology that is finally beginning to be understood. These substances are brought into being whenever we have a thought or emotion; they circulate throughout the body, adhering to every organ system. This is why we must pay attention to our thoughts. There is a *must-see* movie, *What The Bleep Do We Know?!* that illustrates this concept brilliantly. This unique movie was released in 2005, but it is as relevant now as it was then. You may also further explore this phenomenon on the *Gaia* channel.

We are able to shut down production of any neurochemicals that weaken the body's energy-producing and healing capabilities. Because the brain's neurochemical production is controlled by the mind, the balance of mind produces balance of the brain's chemistry, which in turn promotes optimum functioning of the body's energy systems. To create this balance of mind, Dr. Chopra—in virtually every book he's written, and every talk he's ever given—underscores the reduction and elimination of stress.

With more and more women in high stress jobs, it's really no wonder that conception doesn't always occur immediately (disastrous in our *I-Want-It-Right-NOW* society), and "trying" to get pregnant is simply anti-hypnotic. The word try implies failure to the subconscious mind. If a three-year-old *tries* to tie his shoes but can't do it, someone will do it for him. If we *try* to lose weight and don't, the mind eventually realizes that to try does not mean to succeed.

Try is another of those words you'll want to strike from your vocabulary. Spiritual gurus, martial artists—even Yoda (the wise and powerful Jedi Master from Star Wars)—caution against *trying*.

We must not *try*—we must *do*. But there is a caveat in that statement with regard to conceiving, because we can *over*do. We must learn to *be*. In learning to *be* you might phrase things differently: I am *open* to my healthy pregnancy. I am *receptive* to my baby. I am *playing* at becoming pregnant. Be creative. Incorporate words like *loving, allowing, accepting…* Or, you could go straight to *I am becoming pregnant.*

Hypnotherapy helps to reduce stress and increase confidence. My ultimate objective is to help my clients to create balance. What I call *the balance of intention and surrender*. Basically, you take your doer/achiever abilities and channel them into what you *can* do, while at the same time aligning your energies with the receptivity of *be*ing. This, in turn, enables you to maximize your chances of conceiving naturally and/or increases the success of medical assistance.

Approximately 20 percent (though numbers may vary) of women diagnosed with infertility issues are diagnosed with unexplained infertility. I believe the word unexplained is accurate from a conventional medicine standpoint, however, from a hypnotic standpoint I don't believe it is *un*explained at all. *"Happy thoughts create happy molecules, and healthy thoughts create healthy molecules,"* says Deepak Chopra, Wayne Dyer, and virtually every spiritual speaker/author on the planet. As there are numerous books focusing on the teachings of mind/body connection, I will leave it to you to explore any areas of further interest.

***

"As you think, so shall you become."
— Bruce Lee

Spirituality is apparently in vogue these days. I attribute this, in part, to the massive impact the movie *The Secret*, with its emphasis on the law of attraction, has had on the general public over the past 10 years. I recently read an article about a South American Shaman who said that his spiritual retreats have become overrun with technology-and-profit-obsessed Silicon Valley CEOs who fly across the world for the purpose of "spiritual awakening"—which he feels is more accurately described as spiritual networking. Versions of the law of attraction, and various combinations of "universal laws," have always existed, and may be found in religious and spiritual teachings across the globe. Each may be used to impress successful tendencies upon the subconscious mind. I recommend familiarizing yourself with the HF applications of such edicts.

#1: The mind cannot hold two conflicting thoughts at a time. You are the only person who has any control over the nature of your thoughts—you get to choose. It will take some work, and nobody thinks positively all the time. That's okay. The *cancel technique* is an effective method of releasing negative thoughts or patterns, or the unwanted advice or projections of others. As explained earlier: when you catch yourself thinking a negative thought, cancel it out. Use a giant red X or imagine the delete key of a computer. In your mind, say the words CANCEL, CANCEL. Remember to follow up with a positive thought such as *I embrace a healthy, peaceful pregnancy.* You are building new neural pathways.

#2: Thought precedes reality. Whatever you focus on (internal or external in origin) is what you see more of. Intention creates experience. What you think (say) is what you get. Mental images become imprinted, and the subconscious mind simply follows what is, in essence, a blueprint. Creating and reinforcing a positive blueprint through hypnosis results in positive outcomes. Learning to quell negative thinking — regardless of what others think or say — and focusing on positive thought and action allows nature to take its course.

#3: There is a related physical response for every thought or emotion. Thoughts imprinted in the subconscious create a biochemical response within the body. Hence, over a period of time we can influence our own health or illnesses with conditioned responses. What we think on a regular basis becomes our default. Strong negative emotion (e.g. fear, anger, frustration, etc.) triggers the fight or flight response which causes a flood of stressor hormones to be released throughout the body.

Reinforcement of *I'll never have a baby* or *I hate my body* or W*hy me?!!* and other negative or fear-based thinking patterns results in continual stress. The triggering and retriggering of the fight or flight response, and the ensuing chemical reaction, causes the body to fight itself. Which kind of thoughts do you want to have? What do you want your default to be? You can make a difference right now. You can utilize hypnosis techniques to trigger the parasympathetic nervous system, to create an overall state of calm, and to align yourself with a more positive outlook in general.

#4: New programming in the subconscious is more powerful and wins out over past programming when the two are in conflict. The non-reasoning, childlike subconscious cannot distinguish between fact and fantasy. If the illusion is that new information introduced into a situation is for the person's well-being, the subconscious accepts the new programming—right or wrong. This actually comes in handy with respect to fertility-focused hypnotherapy. As subconscious blocks are released, the belief that pregnancy is possible, natural, and even imminent becomes truth. The body has an innate knowing that it can become pregnant. I think of this *knowing* as its own entity and call it the *primal body.* Monitoring your thinking is the best way to make the most of this law of the mind because it can work for you or against you. The inherent knowing the body has that it can become pregnant can be destroyed by information (true or not) to the contrary that is received from any number of sources. A person in a state of vulnerability can easily accept information contrary to her best interest for many reasons. The aura of authority and infallibility of medical personnel can easily cause a sense of hopelessness. Internet surfing, reading negative or fear-based blogs, and incessant *Googling* guarantees you will find all sorts of dreadful news to bring you down. Television programs, news, even advertisements can sucker punch the mind. **XXX** *CANCEL, CANCEL!!!*

#5: Once a thought is accepted and acted upon, behavior becomes easier with each subsequent similar thought. Once a woman becomes aware that being balanced and centered is possible, she more readily accepts this principle and acts accordingly. The conviction becomes stronger with practice. Once a calm relaxed state has been accessed in hypnosis, the mind realizes that it is not necessary to be uptight during the fertility process. The more reinforcement in the form of subsequent hypnosis sessions, self-hypnosis, meditation, yoga, guided imagery, etc., the more and more natural the state of relaxation becomes, and the easier it is to counter stress.

#6: Once a thought is accepted by the subconscious, it remains intact until it is replaced by another. Regardless of information to the contrary, unless the original imprint is released and destroyed, and a new imprint is substituted, a person will continue to harbor the original thought. The original thought is guarded by the critical faculty, which must be addressed in order to effect the desired change. If the subconscious has perceived infertility as a form of protection or necessary punishment, pregnancy will not occur until that imprint has been removed and replaced by an acceptance of pregnancy or some similar positive perception. Subconscious purge (chapter 6) and/or regression to cause (chapter 7) techniques are typically necessary in these cases.

Chapter 10

WHAT'S RELIGION GOT TO DO WITH IT?

*"We need to find God, and he cannot be found in noise
and restlessness. God is the friend of silence. See how
nature — trees, flowers, grass — grows in silence; see the
stars, the moon, and the sun, how they move in silence...
We need silence to be able to touch souls."*
— Mother Teresa

The Catholic Church vehemently disagrees with the practice of IVF. The Mormon Church leaves it up to the individuals concerned. Many religions have opinions about a number of different issues and readers may or may not agree with any given stance. This is not about religious debate, this is vital information that I would be remiss to omit from this book. For example, even if a woman considers herself a non-practicing Catholic, just the knowledge that the church disapproves of IVF can still be enough to create subconscious blocks to fertility. Remember that the first information received by our subconscious minds is accepted as truth, and our religious training often qualifies as one of our first sources of information. Some religions have been known to say: *if we can get'em for the first five years, we'll have 'em forever*. Even if we have consciously decided to choose another spiritual direction, if we have not released those initial ideas, we can become conflicted. Whether we are aware of it or not.

I make no judgments about my clients' spiritual beliefs. I am simply aware that conflict is possible. I adjust my hypnotic work accordingly, based on information provided during the interview. Sometimes my clients are comfortable with their religious beliefs, but quite conflicted because they think it is necessary to pursue medical treatment. If their beliefs clash with the pursuit of something (such as IVF) that *they* truly consider to be wrong, they may be relieved to finally be able to admit to themselves that they don't want to continue. On the other hand, sometimes a client desires to change her subconscious belief to one more in harmony with her current practices, or that supports the medical route she consciously wants to take. I use hypnosis to reinforce the desired outcome — whatever it may be.

I support my clients in their choices, but I encourage them to keep their personal beliefs to themselves. I am not a fan of infertility chat rooms, message boards, and most blogs because — though they may be intended to be supportive — they often do more damage than good. See the article: *The Cheese Stands Alone* in the appendix for more on this topic. Such sites are anti-hypnotic because as you constantly read about people's pain and frustration, and/or failed procedures or miscarriages, etc. you vicariously experience them yourself — over and over and over. Though I've heard arguments to the contrary, such as someone needing support or that sometimes there are positive experiences included as well, with what you now know about the subconscious mind, I'm sure you understand why I think such hard and heavy emotional experiences (whether or not they are your own) can create unwanted blocks to pregnancy.

Update: In the 11 years since the first edition of *It's Conceivable!* was released, I have received countless testaments — from clients, readers, folks who have attended my presentations, medical doctors, therapists, HFTs, other CAM fertility practitioners, and so forth — of how making this one small change has helped immensely with overall mind state. Many women have contacted my office to say that they were pregnant by the time they finished this book, or shortly thereafter, "just because" they had a new understanding, and/or had made a few adjustments. On the flip side, I've seen some women who have not, or will not, let go of such involvements become more and more hopeless, more and more drained, more and more negative.

Unless you have some healthy fertility support, I recommend remaining silent about your fertility experiences. Even though it may be tempting to commiserate with others in similar circumstances, or even feel necessary to share your struggles with friends or family, you are only inciting more heartbreak if they do not — or cannot — provide what you need. Keep in mind that people with an external locus of control, those who believe that their successes or failures are mostly caused by external factors beyond their control (luck, fate, injustice, unfairness...), tend to need more outside support because they feel that others have a lot of influence over their lives. People with an internal locus of control are usually more self-reliant. Knowing in which direction you lean can help you immensely. Discernment, of course, is key.

In his book *Manifest Your Destiny*, Dr. Wayne Dyer lists nine spiritual principles for attaining what you want. The fourth principle is *You Can Attract to Yourself What You Desire*. He addresses the *Value of Secrecy*, telling us that when we speak to others about our efforts to manifest, our power is weakened. Dr. Dyer makes the point that in general, when we describe our activities to others it is because the ego — the piece of us that wants to control everything — has taken center stage, and this kind of approach dissipates our power of attraction considerably.

Although it is human nature to talk to others about problems we want to alleviate (or we are at least hoping that by sharing we'll be able to relieve some of their pressure), when we articulate our power to attract something our attention shifts to the reactions of those in whom we are confiding. Energy is then dispersed in the direction of their reactions in the same way that it is when we share problems, rather than directed toward manifesting our goals. And people may be envious, or judgmental, or insensitive about what you are doing, and that is energetically detrimental to your cause. The moment a thought is presented to another person, it is weakened, says Dr. Dyer. "Maintain privacy concerning your own unique, possibly mysterious-to-others, powers to attract to you what you desire." At the end of the chapter are *Some Ideas for Putting this Principle to Work*: Keep your mental picturing to yourself, so that what you want to attract is a private matter between you and God. Discussing it with others will dissipate the energy in the direction of ego and the opinions of others.

In his book *Inspiration*, Dr. Dyer reinforces the wisdom he has shared with us many times over the past four decades, listing what he calls 6 *Principles for Living an Inspired Life*. This is one of my favorite books. It is definitely a great reinforcement to your new way of thinking. Some of the principles he encourages us to practice — and that I personally live by — include:

- Being independent of the good opinion of others.
- Being willing to accept the disapproval of others.
- Staying detached from outcomes.
- Remembering that our desires won't arrive by our schedule.

Again, these are guidelines presented for your consideration. They are in harmony with the hypnotic principles and laws of the mind mentioned earlier in this book. The more we reinforce positive thinking in our lives, the stronger the neural pathways we create, and the more natural it becomes for us.

Chapter 11

BECOMING THE AUTHOR OF YOUR LIFE STORY

"The thing women have got to learn is that nobody gives you power. You just take it."
— Roseanne

Having used hypnotic techniques in giving birth to my second child in 1995, I am extremely supportive of the power of hypnosis in promoting calmness and comfort for mother, child, and father/partner during the birthing process. I can also speak first-hand about the power of hypnosis for fertility, having conceived my son utilizing some of these very techniques to overcome issues due to a vasectomy reversal which was only partially successful.

"Optimism goes all the way with pessimism but arrives at a point far beyond it." This philosophy is taught by my mentor, Dr. C. Scot

Giles* to persons living with cancer as they progress toward health. The body has a natural tendency toward health and embracing an optimistic outlook supports this re-balancing. Hypnotism is the method of teaching this principle to the mind.

Hormonal problems often contribute to conception issues. Restoration of hormonal balance and eventual pregnancy may occur by utilization of these techniques and implementation of positive lifestyle changes such as diet and exercise. Hypnosis is well recognized for its effectiveness in smoking cessation, weight control, stress and anxiety release, removal of subconscious blocks, and general habit changing. Interestingly, these same issues pose the biggest threat to fertility.

The goal of HypnoFertility® is not simply for you to become pregnant, but rather is to enable you to attain personal empowerment. For only by doing so will you truly be able to let things unfold in just the right time, and in just the right way. Through personal empowerment comes inner peace, the ability to accept, appreciate, and embrace life. The baby, as I always say, is the icing on the cake.

Dr. C. Scot Giles is the creator of the ICAN Program, a hospital based, medically-approved program using hypnotism as an adjunct in the treatment of cancer. It is a cooperative venture of La Grange Memorial Hospital in La Grange, Illinois, and Dr. Giles, and was the first approved program of its kind in America. Patients have been helped since 1991 with spectacular results.

Published outcomes research on this program show that participants have an average ten-year survival that is better than the estimated five-year survival for their cancer when compared to the national cancer outcomes database. To read Dr. Giles' research go to: www.ngh.net and click on downloads or visit his web site: www.csgiles.org.

Laws of the Mind that Effect Change:

#1: Law of Desire: There must be a burning desire for the positive outcome. You must truly want the outcome you claim to seek. Secondary benefit derived from extra attention from family/friends, or a usual behavior of fragility, weakness, and needing help can create an obstacle to conception. Reinforcing belief in yourself as an independent individual can result in a far different outcome.

#2: Law of Harmonious Attraction: This is by far the most important law of thought, and yet, it is one of the most difficult to apply. All that you say (or hear) and believe is what you get. We attract conditions and situations that are in harmony with our thinking. Like attracts like. It is essential that any situation that is not wanted be totally avoided. Leave all negativity to others — DON'T GO THERE!

#3: Law of Belief/Expectancy: Success is achieved only with your trust in yourself and the belief that it can be done. What one expects to happen, inevitably happens.

#4: Law of Relaxation: Also known as the law of opposite effort. If doing manual work, one must put all effort into it. When approaching mental work, one must step aside and let it come naturally. Desired outcomes cannot be forced or manipulated. Imagery is the tool, thought is the technique. Thoughts are things. Thoughts have energy that is the ability to bring about the desired change or circumstance.

#5: Law of Visualization: You must see the positive end result. "Think from the end," as Wayne Dyer teaches. Dr. Joe Dispenza is now famous for his reference to this type of thinking in the movie *What The Bleep Do We Know?!* He has done some fascinating work in this area. Through hypnosis techniques you can be helped to see yourself clearly conceiving.

#6: Law of Substitution: Since the mind can hold only one thought at a time, and you are the person who chooses what that thought will be, it is essential that negative thoughts be immediately canceled, and that empty space be filled with a substituted positive image/statement.

#7: Law of Mental Practice: Daily practice of hypnosis and other techniques such as meditation and yoga reinforce balance of mind/body/spirit. Hypnotic suggestion becomes more powerful with repetition and the more you experience this mind state the more natural it becomes for you.

#8: Law of Self-Concept: You must know that you are deserving and capable of achieving the desired outcome. That you are a mature, decisive, independent, empowered woman who is able to think and choose for herself. If you are constantly subjecting yourself to the negative thoughts of others you will lose faith and trust in yourself and in your body's natural abilities. Negatives must be released, and your strong sense of self-confidence must be at the forefront of your mind. This is your responsibility—no one can do it for you.

There was a song on the radio a few years ago called *Unwritten*, by Natasha Bedingfield. I love this song—it's got a great beat, and the words are truly inspiring. (They actually played it at a Wayne Dyer talk I attended a few years ago.) It really underscores what this chapter is about. I recommend you find it online and have a listen. It's great reinforcement! Here's a snippet of the lyrics:

"I am unwritten/Can't read my mind/I'm undefined
I'm just beginning/The pen's in my hand/Ending
unplanned..."

"…Feel the rain on your skin/No one else can feel it for you/Only you can let it in, no one else/No one else, can speak the words on your lips

Drench yourself in words unspoken/Live your life with arms wide open/Today is, where your book begins… The rest is still unwritten…"

Chapter 12

WHY HYPNOSIS? WHAT MOTIVATED SOME OF THE GREATS?

"Cautious, careful people always casting about to preserve their reputation or social standards never can bring about reform. Those who are really in earnest are willing to be anything or nothing in the world's estimation, and publicly and privately, in season and out, avow their sympathies with despised ideas and their advocates, and bear the consequences."
— Susan B. Anthony

Milton Erickson (1902-1980) has done more than any other individual the 20th century to change the way in which hypnotherapy is practiced. As a boy he suffered from polio so severely that a doctor predicted imminent death. Erickson overheard this and his annoyance with the doctor seems to have helped him to survive the experience, though he remained physically weakened for much of his life and had to spend periods of time in a wheelchair. Told he would never walk again, Erickson spent many hours concentrating his attention on achieving even a hint of movement in the muscles of his legs; he was up walking with crutches within a year. This determination—and its results—drove Erickson to acquire degrees in medicine and psychology, eventually becoming a psychiatrist. He gained experience working in a number of psychiatric institutions, and later as a professor of psychiatry. He was a fellow of many international professional bodies and was the founding president of the American Society for Clinical Hypnosis (ASCH).

Dave Elman's (1900-1967) interest in hypnosis was stimulated at an early age by his father who was an accomplished hypnotist. When Dave was only eight years old he learned of the vast possibilities of hypnosis for pain relief. His father was dying of cancer, and a family friend—a famous hypnotist renowned for performing outstanding feats—used hypnosis to relieve the intractable pain quite rapidly. Dave saw his father wracked with the pain of terminal cancer one minute, then, following a few brief moments of hypnosis, the pain was relieved, and Dave was able visit and play with his dad for a little while.

Dave Elman's father was given relief by a stage hypnotist even though doctors had said there was no way to relieve his suffering. Elman eventually went on to train hundreds of physicians in medical hypnotism from the late 1940s through the early 1960s. Over the course of his career, he honed some powerful inductions and applications that are used to this day.

Perhaps the best-known hypnotist of our modern era, Dave Elman has written extensively about the importance of promoting positive expectations in clients so as to ensure positive outcomes. In particular, in his book, *Hypnotherapy*, Elman details how amazingly successful Dr. Henry Munro, a Midwestern physician practicing around the turn of the 20th century, was in his use of hypnosis to prepare his patients for surgery. Not only did Dr. Monroe use hypnosis to alleviate their stress, but also to provide them with confidence as to the outcome of their procedures, and to reinforce their innate abilities to heal well and rapidly.

According to Elman, Dr. Munro was especially concerned about the incidence of death resulting from the use of chemical anesthesia. Through the use of hypnosis, he was able to dramatically reduce the amount of anesthesia (ether, at that time) his patients required. Dr. Monroe had an excellent record of successful surgeries due to the combination of stress reduction, positive expectations, and low doses of ether he used. Sadly, however, his innovative approach was largely ridiculed by his colleagues.

It was only when Dr. Monroe happened to meet with the Mayo brothers—founders of the world-famous *Mayo Clinic* in Rochester, MN — that he found a receptive audience for his new approach to anesthesia and surgery. The brothers agreed to see if they could duplicate Dr. Munro's methods, and what they achieved was phenomenal. Although it was not widely known that the Mayo brothers were using hypnotic methods, their many successful surgeries drew patients from all over the world.

Although initially attracted to hypnosis for personal reasons, both Elman and Erickson eventually devoted most of their lives to the advancement of hypnosis. Many articles and books have been written about these unprecedented individuals. The only book Elman ever wrote, *Hypnotherapy* (originally published under the title *Findings in Hypnosis*), is used in hypnotherapy trainings and schools almost universally. In 1958, Hypnosis was recognized by the American Medical Association (AMA) as a legitimate, safe approach to medical and psychological problems. Today more people recognize the mind-body connection. Mind and body are integrated parts of a whole being, a change in one part effects the other.

Chapter 13

CASE STUDIES

*"Many persons have a wrong idea of what constitutes
true happiness. It is not attained through self-
gratification but through fidelity
to a worthy purpose."*
— *Helen Keller*

Following are overviews of several case studies from my practice. Some of them were included in the first edition of *It's Conceivable!*, and have been updated. There are also some new ones. I have chosen these women's stories so that you can get a better idea of why people seek hypnosis to enhance fertility, and how it can help.

The women in these cases are not necessarily over the age of 40. That is partly because I want to emphasize that age is not the only issue that can impact fertility. Younger women can face terrible difficulties in trying to get pregnant, often struggling for years. It is not fair to dismiss anyone's pain based on age, diagnosis, whether or not they already have a child, or for any other reason. I see that far too often, and it helps no one.

As with this entire book, the purpose of these case studies is to inspire hope. It is to awaken a broader sense of compassion for ourselves and for others. It is to illustrate what is possible when we learn to let go. It is a reminder to look for the good, to keep gratitude in our hearts, and to be open and receptive.

Charlene

Having experienced three miscarriages and a failed IVF cycle in the past year and a half, 40-year-old Charlene was none too happy to have to start over again. She hated needles and was terrified of having to redo the painful shots necessary for IVF. She also dreaded the side effects which she'd experienced as mood swings, hot flashes, and painful ovaries. She'd been diagnosed with unexplained infertility and felt her time was running out. A successful executive with a strong personality, Charlene was determined to repeat the IVF until she became pregnant, but she was "deathly afraid of needles," as she put it, and the stress was nearly intolerable.

Session #1

I used hypnotic regression to find the experience that caused Charlene's needle phobia. She accessed an experience in a doctor's office at the age of three which we determined to be the source of the problem (ISE). After reframing the experience Charlene felt empowered and liberated. Upon future progression (imagining a positive scene in the future, sometimes referred to as *mental rehearsal*), she was happy to find that she wasn't at all bothered by needles and that she could imagine herself with several healthy babies.

Session #2

Charlene's second session focused on the healthy stimulation of her ovaries and production of viable eggs. Her doctor's goal was six to ten eggs. She happily reported she had experienced only the mildest symptoms from the hormone injections in the past week, no mood swings at all, and no more needle problems! After hypnotizing Charlene, I utilized a subconscious purge (designed to clear her subconscious mind of negative thoughts, beliefs, and expectations), and then spent some time connecting her to a successful point of reference. For hypnotic purposes, connecting with a point of reference means tapping into a previous success and utilizing the positive emotion accessed therein.

We used the metaphor of a blueprint to set a strong foundation for a successful pregnancy.

Session #3

Charlene reported that the doctor said all was going very well. There were more follicles than expected for Charlene's age. Even though she was "living from one ultrasound to the next," Charlene was impressed that she was not uptight about everything the way she had been previously. Hypnotic reinforcement reminded her body that it knew what to do—that all was well. Charlene went inside and embraced her ovaries, gave them a pep talk, and encouraged them to produce strong, healthy eggs.

Session #4

Charlene's retrieval was successful. The doctors had thought they might get nine eggs; they retrieved fifteen. Her mood was great. She had been practicing self-hypnosis and tapping into her subconscious, envisioning her womb as soft, inviting, full of life, and welcoming her babies. Charlene had had a fresh transfer of three embryos, and she and her husband were hoping for twins, or even triplets.

After a rapid induction (a hypnotic technique which produces trance in less than three minutes), I used hypnotic suggestion techniques to reinforce Charlene's positive experiences. She also connected with her inner assistant (see below), who assured Charlene that everything was ready and that she, the inner assistant, would take good care of the babies. A subconscious purge to address any residual fears of past miscarriages/disappointment completed the session.

Session #5

Charlene was thrilled to be five weeks pregnant. She was feeling good, a little tired which her doctor had said was quite normal. She had continued with her stress reduction recording and visualizations at home.

A rapid hypnosis induction was followed by an opportunity to check in with her inner assistant (Charlene's assistant was a teeny, tiny nurse). Her nurse told her that she worried too much and advised her to check in more often and she'd feel better. Communicating with her body, Charlene visualized her embryos as tiny babies, seat-belted into her uterus. She took a pleasant journey through an enchanted forest. There, Charlene relaxed in an energetic healing pool and connected with her inner goddess—her purest form of self. During her future progression Charlene reported that she had given birth and was holding her healthy babies. That it was all behind them now!

Charlene continued with pregnancy support — mainly for comfort — and she utilized hypnosis for her birth. She was scheduled for a mandatory cesarean-section as is often the case with multiples. Hypnosis supports both vaginal and surgical birth, facilitating a gentler, more peaceful experience, and aiding in quicker recovery.

Charlene gave birth to three baby girls a few months later — right on schedule. I caught up with her a few years after the first edition of *It's Conceivable!* was released, her kids were about seven years old by then. Charlene said that everyone was plugging along happy and healthy. She told me that she was still so thrilled at how helpful the hypnosis had been that she tells anyone who will listen. She also mentioned that she and the girls had experienced "next to none" of the expected issues that can accompany a multiple pregnancy, and there were no developmental delays in any of the children. Charlene said she totally attributes that to the hypnosis.

Multiples are quite common in my practice. Over the years there have been several sets of triplets, and countless sets of twins. *Irish Twins* (colloquialism for siblings born less than 12 months apart) tend to show up a lot as many of my clients conceive naturally (and easily) once they have given birth to their first baby(s). I caution my clients to use birth control, or at least be careful, if they don't want another baby too soon. Yes, they look at me like I'm crazy — but I'm the one who frequently gets the news that there is another *unexpected* baby on the way. So, I throw that out there to them, and to you.

The *inner assistant* is a powerful technique during which my client enters her inner world and meets with a being (sometimes a nurse, doctor, midwife, angel, guide... often it's a friend or relative who has passed on) that resides within her uterus. This being represents her own inner knowing or intuition and provides her with great comfort over the upcoming days, weeks, months, and empowering her to participate in her own experience. Many of my clients have emerged from hypnosis excitedly reporting that their inner assistant has assured them that everything is functioning properly, that they are not alone, that he/she/it is on the job. The incredible accuracy of the inner assistant illustrates how strong our own inner knowing is, and how important it is to trust our feelings.

Several of my clients and students with endometriosis have reported, independently, that when they went into their uterus, they found their inner nurse/assistant scraping wallpaper and repainting the room (womb). Remember: the subconscious mind responds to pictures, imagery, metaphor. Though it may seem a little silly — which is a conscious mind judgment — this interactive visualization is highly effective.

The *enchanted forest* and the *healing pool* are other metaphors I use. Both are excellent for subconscious purging, and each provides a wonderful opportunity for strengthening and rebuilding self-confidence. They may also facilitate a connection with the inner voice or higher self.

*A free download of the healing pool fertility journey is available on my website: www.hypnofertility.com

***

Beth

39-year-old Beth had been diagnosed with secondary infertility. She had been to a reproductive endocrinologist who had informed her that her FSH was too high, and that she had poor egg quality. Although she had been scheduled for IVF, her doctor cancelled the procedure after these unexpected test results had come back, telling her he would reconsider IVF if her FSH levels lowered, but not to count on it.

Beth decided to seek out hypnosis to try to lower her FSH numbers which had more than tripled in the span of just a few months. Her goal was to normalize the hormone levels, so the doctor would then attempt the IVF. Time was of the essence and we began immediately. I wanted to get at least four sessions in with Beth before she went back for subsequent testing.

During the first session I helped Beth access her control room and make adjustments to her hormone levels. She also went in and checked on her egg quality, which she found to be quite good despite medical advice to the contrary. Beth selected a plump, healthy egg from her stash, reminding herself that she only needed one. It only takes one good egg to create a healthy baby. I reconnected Beth with a successful point of reference from her past. Because she'd already had a successful pregnancy, I used hypnotic suggestion to remind her subconscious mind of her previous pregnancy and reestablish the pregnancy goal. (This technique is also effective for women with primary infertility, we simply use a different accomplishment as the point of reference.)

To achieve maximum hypnotic benefit in the shortest amount of time — the more time spent in *rest and digest*, the better — I had Beth work with a stress reduction CD every day between sessions with me. ****These days, thanks to some awesome technology that wasn't available when I worked with Beth in 2003, I am able to provide more specific reinforcement recordings that clients can easily access on their smartphones anytime they wish.*

Abuse issues disclosed during the interview were released both through subconscious purge and hypnotic regression. On her first session I also had Beth do a set of drawings (I sometimes use drawing analysis for subconscious access) which gave me some specific insight into her subconscious state. I was pleased to find the overall state of her drawings to be pleasant, and it seemed we would have a positive outcome.

On the morning of her fourth session, Beth excitedly told me her news: she was pregnant! Before she could even have her FSH retested, before the possibility of IVF could be revisited, Beth was naturally pregnant. A few months later Beth came in to learn hypnosis for birth, so she could have the satisfying natural birth experience she had always dreamed of. Her daughter was born in early 2004.

I saw Beth occasionally through her pregnancy, then for four hypnosis birthing sessions during her last trimester. She wanted to tandem nurse until her babies naturally weaned, so we also reinforced lactation.

***

Allison

Allison was 28 years old when she booked her first HypnoFertility® session with me. She had a child from her first marriage but had been unable to get pregnant during the past four years with her new husband. Her doctor had diagnosed her with unexplained infertility. Allison was devastated. At least, by her way of thinking, if there was a medical diagnosis, a physiological *("real")* reason, something could be done about it. There would be a medicine, a surgery, something that would remedy the situation. But unexplained? To Allison that meant there was absolutely nothing she could do, nothing the doctors could do.

Allison was depressed and frustrated. She had pursued medical treatment because she wanted to *do* something. By the time I saw her, Allison had spent a lot of money and time trying to get pregnant. Sex had become a chore. The fertility drugs had made her sick and she had gained a lot of weight. The intrauterine inseminations (IUI) were painful and she was certain that in vitro fertilization (IVF) would be worse—and even more expensive. She was about ready to give up on her dream of having another baby.

During the intake Allison told me she'd had an abortion since giving birth to her first child. Her first husband had been abusive. He was a drug addict and didn't work. She could barely take care of her first child let alone have another one. She had driven herself to the abortion clinic, and then tried to forget about it. But she hadn't forgotten; she'd just buried it in her subconscious.

Session #1

During her first hypnosis session I assisted Allison in establishing a safe place in her mind. She visited her womb, accessed her inner assistant, and made sure everything was ready for the new baby. I gave her a stress reduction CD and instructed her to listen to it daily between this and her second session, at which point I would do a regression to resolve the abortion issue.

Session #2

Allison reported that she was feeling a lot better, more in balance, since her first session. Regressions can take a great deal of time, so we got right to work. Following a rapid induction, I regressed Allison back to the abortion experience. In cases where there is a specific abortion or miscarriage incident that needs to be resolved, I am not necessarily looking for an SSE-ISE event chain. My goal is to commune with the baby(s). In trance her baby appeared before her. *A very brief overview of the regression is transcribed below:*

Lynsi: What's happening?

Allison: My baby, my sweet baby is here. He is so serene. My baby is at peace. I'm so sorry. I'm sorry my baby. I didn't mean to hurt you. (Sobbing.)

L: Would you like to ask your baby for forgiveness? Not in the religious sense, but in a way that will release you from this terrible guilt?

When we speak of forgiveness for hypnosis purposes, we are not talking about the religious sense of forgiveness. A lot of times just mentioning the word triggers an instant resistance in people who have negative religious connotations with it, or associate forgiveness with words like deserve and/or punish. Any time that forgiveness is brought up in hypnotherapy, it is done so with a statement similar to the one I used with Allison: "Not in the religious sense, but for your benefit/in a way that will release you from the self-inflicted bonds of guilt that enslave you/for clarity and understanding..."

A: Yes. He forgives me! He says it's all right. It was supposed to be this way. He says to forgive myself. He is okay. He is sending another baby to me. A boy! I'm not a bad person, he understands, and it is okay. I'm holding him now. His heart against my heart. He is always with me.

The interaction with aborted or miscarried babies is a form of a hypnosis technique known as Gestalt. *Hypnotic gestalt is not the same as psychiatric* Gestalt Therapy *such as that of Fritz Perls. I sometimes refer to this technique as my* Rapid Conception Technique, *because it very often results in immediate pregnancy. It is not usually done on the second session, but in Allison's case it was appropriate.*

L: Is there anything else at this time?

A: No, this issue is resolved.

L: Move forward in time now, a few months, a year or so. What's happening?

A: I am pregnant! I can feel my baby moving within me. Now, I've given birth—I'm holding my baby, he is healthy. He is beautiful.

Allison conceived her baby naturally not long after her session with her *Spirit Baby*. About five months after Allison's second session she dropped in on a seminar I was giving to show me her pregnant belly. Her son (remember her spirit baby told her he was sending her a boy) was born with the use of hypno birth less than a year after that first session. A second little boy came naturally—and unexpectedly—about a year and a half later.

Personally, I believe that the greatest spiritual growth occurs as we learn to forgive—ourselves and others—without judgment. That's not an easy thing to do. Should you feel that forgiveness work would be beneficial to you, hypnosis can be quite helpful. Even if we think (consciously) that we don't need forgiveness, or that we don't want or need to forgive anyone, the subconscious mind's interpretation of forgiveness may not be in alignment with what we think. This misalignment could also contribute to a subconscious block.

***

Rachel

41-year-old Rachel came in to see me a couple of years ago. She had just experienced her second failed embryo transfer and had been told by her doctor that she needed to take six months to address some health problems before they would transfer her final two embryos. Rachel was devastated, but she had resigned herself to do what she had been directed to do. Rachel had first been alerted to potential fertility issues when she'd been diagnosed with pelvic inflammatory disease (PID) at age 37. Tests had revealed some scarring on her fallopian tubes, which, her doctor had told her, could make it difficult for her to conceive naturally. Not being ready to start a family at the time, Rachel had put the issue out of her mind.

When Rachel was 39 years old, she and her husband began actively trying to conceive. After a few months without success, she remembered what her doctor had said a couple of years earlier following her PID episode. She immediately went to a fertility clinic for an evaluation. The results of her workup found that Rachel had low AMH and high

FSH, in addition to her other issue. Rachel was told that it was extremely unlikely that she would be able to get pregnant naturally and with her age, tube damage, and poor FSH and AMH levels, was advised to do IVF with donor eggs. The recommendation of donor eggs was more than Rachel and her husband could bear. They left the clinic in tears and went home to regroup.

Rachel could not shake the sense of urgency instilled by the doctor, but neither she nor her husband could reconcile the idea of donor eggs. They elected to start right away with IVF, but insisted they at least try with Rachel's own eggs. Her first cycle ended up being canceled because she didn't have enough eggs. She had only two follicles the second cycle, so it was downgraded to an IUI, which was not successful. Next, a new and more aggressive protocol resulted in six eggs retrieved, four fertilized. Two embryos survived.

Another stim cycle was decided on with the hopes of increasing Rachel's chances. The purpose of repeated stim cycles is to, ideally, be able to "bank" or "stockpile" several embryos which can then be sent for pre-implantation genetic diagnosis or screening (PGD, PGS respectively), and/or used for subsequent embryo transfers. Back-to-back stim cycles are typically done for "poor responders" or in cases of delayed childbearing. Because genetic testing is so expensive, many people prefer to get as many embryos as possible and send them to the lab all at once. And, of course, the chances of having healthy embryos are presumed to be increased simply due to quantity.

After three back-to-back stim cycles in all, Rachel had a grand total of four frozen embryos. One embryo was transferred the first time, with no success. After a break of a couple months, the doctor (who had determined the transfer of two embryos to be too risky in Rachel's case) transferred the second of her four embryos. This frozen embryo transfer (FET) also failed, and it was at this point that Rachel came to see me.

Rachel was less than optimistic about her chances of becoming a mother after all that she had been through. During her initial intake, I learned (beyond what is mentioned above) that infidelity had proven to have contributed to the initial issue of PID, and that her marriage had barely survived. As it turned out, both Rachel and her husband had confessed to infidelity, and each one—having no idea that the other one had also had an affair—had assumed that they had been responsible for causing the infection, and had been unable to carry the guilt. However, the fact that each of them had cheated on the other did little to ease feelings of guilt, shame, and blame for either of them.

In the end, they had forgiven each other and resolved to move forward. Rachel said she truly did feel that things had improved, and that she and her husband were more in tune with one another. That their marriage was stronger, and that they had grown closer in spite of—or perhaps because of—it all. They had decided it was time to have a family. A few months later their dreams were dashed with the infertility confirmation. In their minds, *they deserved it. It was their punishment, of course, for the sin of adultery.*

I have no judgment about people in such cases. No one is perfect. Mistakes are lessons; lessons lead to improvements, healing, and opportunities for growth. I have found that when there is infidelity in a marriage, there is a reason for it. It's never black and white — no matter who the victim is or appears to be. (I'm not talking victim blaming or shaming, I am referring to holding a non-threatening space so that whatever needs to come up or come out can do so in a place of absolute safety.) I don't condone it, nor do I judge it. From my standpoint, it just is what it is, and it's a place to begin. (Or, at least, to consider.) Rachel and I worked together for 15 sessions. During that time, she became pregnant and eventually gave birth to a healthy, handsome little boy.

It may seem that the infidelity would be the crux of this case, but it was not. Nor was Rachel's medical diagnosis. I did not need to do a regression to cause — although the severity of the presenting issues might seem, upon first glance, to indicate that one would be necessary. (See below for an overview of Rachel's sessions.) The first session is always a release and a relief. It's almost as though my clients take one deep breath, and then talk for an hour and half. And let it all out. I listen. That's what I do. I don't need a lot of detail; I basically want an overview of what you have been dealing with.

The throes of *in*fertility can be very isolating. Friends and family don't always understand, or they have no idea what to do or how to support you. People constantly offer advice and/or insensitive comments. You are subjected to pregnancy announcements, birth announcements, baby shower invitations, gender-reveal parties, babies on television, babies in movies, babies in restaurants... pregnant women in the stores — sometimes toting a toddler or two, pregnant women at work, pregnant women on the street... As I mentioned earlier, the subconscious mind is goal-achieving. It knows you want a baby, so it's *helping* you: babies and pregnant women are everywhere you turn.

Some people elect to share everything with everyone. Sometimes this works out, and sometimes they deeply regret it as every single day they are inundated with texts and phone calls and e-mail follow-ups. This is especially difficult when something doesn't go as planned. Others keep their fertility travails to themselves. This sometimes creates distance that doesn't transcend its reason. Friendships are damaged, families are distressed. Marriages may be strained, although a fertility crisis can also strengthen the bond and bring the couple closer. Regardless, men don't typically have the emotional stamina of women, and are not always capable of handling a woman's struggle or supporting her to the level she needs. And men like to fix things.

Fertility issues are extremely difficult for men to deal with because they can't stand to see their partners hurting, but they can't fix anything. They might avoid the topic so that they don't upset you. Or change the subject. Or try to distract you. Or tell you not to cry. But, to most women, these tactics are anything but kind, and certainly not supportive.

Doctors have limited time to spend with their patients, and you can end up feeling like not much more than a number. And certainly not heard, not validated. On top of that, running all over the place for appointments and treatments and tests becomes a fulltime job. It is frustrating, and it is exhausting. So much to do, so much rushing. No wonder people feel unsupported.

I spend a lot of time with my clients, and while they are with me, they are my only concern. Doctors have very little time to spend with patients, and for a lot of their appointments, women don't even get to see the doctor. Much medical communication is handled by e-mail or phone tag/voicemails with nurses. Chiropractic treatment just does not take a lot of time, so it really doesn't provide an atmosphere for intimate discussion. You might get more interaction with your acupuncturist, but many of them alternate two or more rooms at once so can't spend lengthy amounts of time with their patients. And it is not necessary for effective treatment in any of these circumstances.

Hypnosis, as I like to think of it, is the missing link. It is not contraindicated to anything — medical or alternative treatments, nutrition, exercise, meditation. It complements, it supports, and it enhances anything else you may be doing. What you need is a team. Whatever practitioners, whatever treatments you decide to choose, all comprise your team. Hypnosis weaves a subconscious tapestry of the benefits of each. The mind/body/spirit balance provides the receptive environment essential to conception.

Session #1

Balance is my ultimate focus for fertility clients. Balance of mind/body/spirit, balance of systems of the body, balance of right and left brain thinking. Balance of intention and surrender. I used a deep hypnosis technique to access Rachel's subconscious mind, bypassing the chaos of her thinking self, triggering her parasympathetic nervous system, and establishing a calm and peaceful state of being. She had barely opened her eyes before she began telling me how wonderful the hypnosis was, and how she had not felt so at ease in such a long time.

Session #2

Rachel reported that she'd felt more hopeful between her first session and this one. She could see more clearly, and not be so hard on herself. That said, she told me she definitely needed to lose some weight (about 50 lbs.) and asked if I could help her with that.

Hypnosis is extremely effective for weight loss. Studies have shown people using hypnosis along with healthy eating and exercise to have lost twice the amount of weight as those just eating healthfully and exercising. Weight gain/loss is not independent of fertility hypnosis. Nor is difficulty sleeping. Or public speaking, for that matter. Anything that is affecting you/your life, anything that is causing stress or worry, can be addressed right along with your presenting issue. Hypnosis can help you stop drinking coffee or wine, stick with any given diet you have been prescribed (gluten-free, dairy-free, sugar-free...), stop smoking, drink more water, exercise more (or less)... basically we can work with anything that may be impeding your success.

The focus of Rachel's second session was weight loss and self-confidence. Diminished self-confidence is pretty standard with fertility clients and must be addressed. Weight issues can also damage confidence and self-esteem. Combined, a woman can feel so overwhelmed that she becomes consumed with beating up and berating herself.

Session #3

Rachel was doing well with her weight loss. She had chosen an eating plan that was recommended to her and that she likes. She had been going to the gym. It had only been a week, but she was thrilled to have lost three pounds. She told me that she was much happier and felt better about herself.

Sessions #4 – 9

As Rachel's self-esteem improved, she was able to confront other fears and frustrations along her fertility journey. I used a hemispheric brain balancing technique to help her tap into her creativity. You cannot left-brain a baby. She was learning to let go more, to allow. To *be*. To stop trying so hard to *do*. Her weight loss was progressing. A subconscious purge helped her to release any obstacles interfering with pregnancy. Her inner assistant had given her some insight and she had prepared her womb room for her upcoming FET—still a few months away. Rachel reported that her intuition was much clearer.

Session #10

Rachel is three months pregnant! She hadn't noticed. Her period had not shown up, but she was so focused on getting ready for her FET that she hadn't been paying any attention to her cycle. She was much more relaxed, she had lost 30 pounds, her relationship was much better. And, of course, she and her husband were thrilled to be expecting their first child.

Session #11 and Beyond...

Rachel had not lost all the weight she had wanted to by the time she found out she was pregnant. In these circumstances I use a hypnotic process designed to redistribute the weight. In other words, if a person is 20 pounds overweight when she gets pregnant, rather than gaining 30 pounds on top of the 20 she is already carrying (virtually equaling a 50-lb gain), hypnosis helps the body to utilize the weight it has, resulting in a total of 30 (ish) pregnancy pounds. (The number of pounds I used is for example purposes only. Healthy pregnancy weight gain varies by height, body type, etc., and should be evaluated by a medical professional on a case-by-case basis.)

I worked with Rachel throughout her pregnancy and, at about 34 weeks, we began hypnosis birth sessions. She gave birth to an adorable baby boy. She did some follow-up weight loss hypnosis and lost most of her pregnancy weight within six months.

Rachel did not end up using IVF to conceive her son. She is enjoying her baby, and I still see her from time to time. Rachel says she's happy to know that if she decides she wants to have more children, she has options.

***

Josie

Josie had been through eight IUIs in about as many months. She had been diagnosed with unexplained infertility. She was 28 years old. Josie and her husband had decided to try one more IUI, they were unsure of what they would do if it did not work. Josie told me that she was hoping that the hypnosis would help her be successful this time, so that she and her husband wouldn't have to consider anything further.

Josie came in for her first appointment just a few days before the insemination would take place. I would have preferred to have had more time to work with her, but I didn't. I'd just have to make the best of the one session I was going to have time for. I don't usually accept clients for just one session, but in this case, I made an exception.

During her intake I discovered that Josie had been raped in college. It had been a date rape, and no one had believed her. The rapist had gotten away with what he had done, and Josie had berated herself constantly for having been so stupid in the first place. I did a regression with Josie to address the rape. Because of the nature of the subconscious mind, the details of the experience are really not important. Once again, what is important is the mind's perception of what happened.

Josie thought she had already processed the rape through traditional therapy, but upon regression, she discovered that not only had she not processed it, she had been absolutely battering herself emotionally because of it. Josie had (subconsciously) decided that *she was not sexually responsible since she had let such a terrible thing happen*, and had, in effect, imposed what she called a "lock down" on her reproductive system to punish herself for her carelessness.

After reframing the incident, Josie was able to show herself some compassion. The rapist was appropriately dealt with through the hypnotic process, and Josie was finally able to release the whole frightening experience. Josie called a few weeks later to tell us her IUI had been successful.

Update: Josie gave birth to a healthy little boy, and she and her husband were able to build their family naturally from that point forward.

***

Lisa

Lisa was 47 years old and had recently transferred her final frozen embryo. She had conceived her daughter naturally seven years earlier. Unable to conceive again, she and her husband had undergone IVF. This had not gone well for Lisa, and after three failed transfers it had taken her nearly five years to "get up the nerve," as she put it, to transfer the last biological embryo she would ever have. Her worst fears came to light, and the FET failed. But Lisa still felt that *she had a baby there* and wanted to bring her baby into this world.

Lisa was a distance client—she lived clear across the country. When I met her, she was at a place where she knew that if she wanted to give birth to another baby, she would need to use donor eggs. This was devastating to her. We worked through her anxiety and angst, and Lisa benefited greatly from the deep hypnosis states she utilized daily. I saw her once per week by *Skype*, and during her fertility hypnosis work with me she was able to release fears and blocks related to having a donor egg baby.

Lisa was concerned about what to say to people. Should she tell people that her child was from a donor egg? What would she tell the child? What would she tell her other children? (Lisa had a biological daughter as well as two older stepchildren.)

Lisa's anxiety levels were excessive when we first began to work together. As time went on, she elected to use a clinic in Denver to pursue a donor cycle. I was able to meet with Lisa personally a few times during her visits to the Denver clinic. The hypnosis enabled Lisa to cultivate, and maintain, a positive attitude about the decision she'd come to, and helped her to choose the correct donor — the donor whose energy was the right fit for her family — from a balanced mind/body/spirit state.

Lisa's donor cycle unfolded beautifully, and her hypnotherapy sessions helped her to remain positive. Hypnosis also helps to create a sense of receptivity so that the baby enters a welcoming environment that is not marred by constant doubt and fear. Lisa's inner assistant gave her a thumbs-up each time she visited her womb. The first time she entered her womb Lisa was pleased to see that it was in pristine shape, just as her little daughter had left it. She made a few adjustments for the new baby, and her inner assistant took care of the rest.

The donor transfer was successful. Lisa was happy that she and her husband were able to choose the gender of the baby. They decided on a little girl so that their daughter would have a little sister. The older boys were thrilled about that decision too. The baby's impending birth was the height of the summer for the family.

Lisa and I worked together throughout her pregnancy and used hypnosis to design and establish this baby's unique birth experience. Each baby is different, and to really emphasize that subconsciously is beneficial, especially after someone has gone through the trauma of so many years of struggle. If a client encountered any complications during the birth of her first child, I make sure to clear them so that they do not interfere with the second. If her first birth experience was positive, the ceaseless stress and anxiety endured through years of disappointment and devastation can obliterate what would, under different circumstances, serve as a nice template for a mom's second birth.

Zoe entered the world in a calm and peaceful environment. A couple of weeks later Lisa and I set up a Skype session so that I could meet the baby. Lisa was just glowing as she showed off her little darling. Lisa told me to please let my clients know that though she was nervous about using donor eggs, though she was afraid she might not love this baby as much as her first child, that her fears were nothing but "left brain interference." *My baby is my baby, and that is THAT!*

Whether she will tell others or not, what she will say to her child, and whether or not she should say anything at all—all of it is moot, Lisa emphasized. The baby had been with Lisa all along—in spirit baby form—she had only wanted to join her family.

Many people are shaken to the core by even the suggestion of using donor eggs. That is understandable, especially when it is prematurely suggested, and other options have not even been considered. I include this case because it is important, and it is valid. Lots of times women have the pre-conceived notion of how they will become pregnant, and exactly what they will or will not do. Sometimes it changes.

What is important is that if a new direction is chosen, that it is undertaken from a place of mind/body/spirit balance, that it comes from a place of clarity, of intuitive *knowing*. Not because of fear. Not from some desperate or knee-jerk reaction.

It is essential to stay in the moment and not run miles ahead trying to control every possibility that might occur. It is the fear of the unknown that continually reinforces the high levels of stress that, in turn, interfere with conception in the first place. The only regret she had, Lisa said, was that she had waited so long to move forward with transferring her last embryo, coming to terms with its loss, and moving forward with her healthy pregnancy and the birth of her sweet little girl.

***

"Don't compromise yourself. You are all you've got."
— Janis Joplin

Chapter 14

CREATING YOUR REALITY

"I believe that imagination is stronger than knowledge.
That myth is more potent than history.
That dreams are more powerful than facts.
That hope always triumphs over experience.
That laughter is the only cure for grief.
And I believe that love is stronger than death."
— Robert Fulghum

Everything, including a baby, starts with an idea. We cannot create something unless we can first imagine it. Ideas become reality once we energize them, once we add emotional energy. Studies have shown that the emotion accompanying an idea or image causes an idea or image to realize itself—the more emotion, the faster the idea becomes reality.

Throughout the pages of this book, I have referenced the late Dr. Wayne Dyer several times. I love to read spiritual and motivational types of books, and I have mentioned a number of them here. Wayne Dyer is my ultimate favorite, and I have spent many pleasant hours poring over his works, watching him on PBS, and listening to him in my car. I have recommended some of his writings and lectures to my clients as a supplement to the work we are doing with hypnosis.

Dr. Dyer often talks about the right people and the right things showing up when we are aligned with Spirit. Interestingly, as I was in the midst of completing this book in 2006, Dr. Dyer's latest book *Inspiration* found its way into my hands. In *Inspiration* Dr. Dyer writes of his own personal hypnosis session where he regressed to a time before he entered this lifetime as Wayne Dyer. This took place so that he might have a conversation with God and find out his purpose for this lifetime. He outlines his own regression in the book and recommends that his readers follow his example and find a way to have the experience themselves.

I had not set out to become a specialist in hypnosis for fertility. The Universe pretty much dumped it in my lap in the early 2000s — and it was up to me to say yes or no. I definitely loved helping women to have babies, and the results I was seeing were intriguing. But, was this actually what I was supposed to do with my life? I knew that once I published my book there would be no turning back (in hindsight, after writing a second book, *The 3 Keys to Conception,* and with a third book soon to be released — not to mention the second edition of *It's Conceivable!* — I can say I was absolutely right about that!), that this would be my life's work, so I needed to know that I should proceed.

As a certified hypnotherapist, I had been facilitating this type of regression work for many years. I call it life purpose regression (LPR). As an empath, I'd become aware of a powerful energetic shift occurring in the world. (Its continued impact upon my fertility hypnosis work is detailed in my third book, *Waiting in the Wings*). I decided to have Amber, Liam's mom, who was working at my office at the time, facilitate a life purpose regression for me. What I experienced was astounding.

Due to all the "coincidences" (I don't believe in coincidence) that seemed to be guiding me, I knew that the outline of my LPR needed to be included in this book. As it turns out, 11 years later, I can see exactly why. Hypnosis is an art and a science; there is also a spiritual component. The significance of the spiritual aspect has become increasingly apparent over the years.

During the LPR, the person is guided to an energetic place (for lack of a better term) — the space we were in before we entered our current body and our current lifetime. I like to call it *The Between*. The Between is also where spirit babies reside. I have found everyone experiences the Between in various ways, yet what is consistent is an immense sense of peace and love.

Upon finding myself in the Between, I became aware of that familiar sense of incredible peace and love. I didn't experience a one-on-one conversation with God per se, as Wayne Dyer did, however, I found myself in a library of sorts, with many large, old books…

Amber: What's happening?

Lynsi: Waves of energy, huge power waves. It's grey, soft, peaceful, loving. Brilliant light. Oh! You can be there and here. You forget when you come here but you can be there and here. You are always connected. It's like the periscope on a submarine. You are actually under water, but you can pop up and see what's above. You can do that here too. There's no time. You can go anywhere, there is no particular order. You don't have to go forward. You get healing here, so you can just know.

A: What are you aware of?

L: Books. Many, many books.

A: Are you aware of your purpose?

L: Recording, writing, teaching… rewriting… Oh! Show people they can overcome the past…

A: Is this your life purpose?

L: Partly. Goodness. I am a gift of goodness to my dad. He had a hard time. My grandfather was mean, violent. He left right after I came in (was born). It was time for my dad to have goodness. I am goodness. I forgot when I came through. I remember now.

A: What's happening now?

L: My book! It's right here in the library. And so is *Inspiration*. It's shifting now. I'm in what seems like a different room. It's full of babies! Babies are a gift of goodness! Liam is there and he's holding a butterfly. I'm getting something: the consciousness has changed. Some kind of lower energies or something. There's not enough babies coming through. But they're there. They say they're always there, but the alignment is off. That's why the moms always feel them—they are there! But out of alignment. The energy is off. Love them, always love them.

A: Anything else?

L: The gift of goodness. Babies are the gift of goodness. It's never too late to recognize the goodness. Anyone can choose.

A: Is there anything else you need to do with this scene?

L: One of the babies is placing itself inside the belly of one of my clients. I'm watching it happen. An easy, gentle shift… and the baby is there.

Amber concluded the LPR at this point. As she emerged me from hypnosis, I was in awe of the feelings I'd experienced. The sense of goodness I'd remembered was palpable. I'd always known the babies were there, yet now I'd actually seen it. When, during the LPR, I saw Liam showing me a butterfly, I knew that getting the book finished was priority, that in writing this book I truly was fulfilling my purpose.

ABOUT THE AUTHOR

I don't go by the rulebook...
I lead from the heart, not the head.
— Princess Diana

Lynsi Eastburn, MA is a registered psychotherapist with the state of Colorado. She is a Board Certified Hypnotherapist (BCH), and Certified Instructor (CI) through the National Guild of Hypnotists (NGH). Lynsi is co-owner and instructor — along with her husband, Drake — of the Eastburn Hypnotherapy Clinic and Eastburn Institute of Hypnotherapy in Colorado, an adjunct faculty member of several hypnosis organizations, and also runs a fulltime private practice with a global clientele.

Lynsi is the creator of HypnoFertility® — a program based on clinical experience gleaned from thousands of hours in her Colorado private practice. She has taught her methods internationally. Lynsi is the recipient of multiple awards — including the *Education and Literature Award* (HBI, 2005) and the National Guild of Hypnotists' prestigious *Hypnosis Research Award* (2005) — for her groundbreaking work in the fertility hypnosis field. Lynsi and Drake were the first hypnosis couple to ever be featured on the cover of *The Journal of Hypnotism* (December 2009), and in 2015 Lynsi was inducted into the esteemed *Order of Braid Council*, NGH, in recognition of "a lifetime of outstanding achievement, dedication, and service."

Lynsi is the author of *It's Conceivable! Hypnosis for Fertility*, an unprecedented book chronicling the development of her process and various success stories of her private clients. Her second book, *The 3 Keys to Conception – Pregnancy Against All Odds*, documenting the evolution of her work, was released in February 2013. The second edition of *It's Conceivable!* was released in the summer of 2017.

In 2016, Lynsi completed her formal research study of hypnosis as a viable treatment for infertility. The results of her research have been published in the second edition of *It's Conceivable!* and in various other publications.

Lynsi's books and research are currently being translated into Hebrew, German, Japanese, and Spanish. Lynsi's third book, *Waiting in the Wings – Introducing the Pink StarLights*, is currently in the works, and is due to be released in 2019.

Originally from Toronto, Canada, Lynsi currently lives in Colorado with her husband Drake and dog Boo Radley. Sadly, their other beloved dog, Scout — Boo's partner in crime — passed away in April 2018 leaving a gaping hole in their otherwise peaceful existence.

Lynsi's oldest son, Kelly, is also a certified hypnotherapist. He has a private practice in Toronto. Her other son, Dylan, is working on his master's degree in music (percussion) at Wichita State University in Kansas.

Lynsi will soon have a new daughter-in-law, Marina. Marina is an opera singer and is also working on her master's degree at Wichita (with Dylan).

Lynsi loves to read, to explore and enjoy meditative practices, and she loves animals. She spends a few hours each week walking and caring for dogs at the local animal shelter.

APPENDIX

IS HYPNOSIS A VIABLE TREATMENT FOR INFERTILITY — A GROUNDED THEORY

Eastburn, Lynsi, MA
Board Certified Clinical Hypnotherapist
Certified Hypnosis Instructor

Abstract

The objective of this study was to establish the efficacy of hypnosis as a viable treatment for infertility in women. The study was prompted by a vast accumulation of anecdotal evidence; and based on 36 client case studies — spanning a 15-year period — attained from the private files of the researcher, a clinical hypnotherapist specializing in infertility hypnosis. Files pertaining exclusively to female clients whose hypnosis treatment resulted in both conception and live birth(s) were reviewed. Notable results included that 88.88% of clients were self-proclaimed "Type-A" personalities, and 100% of clients reported significant improvement following the first hypnosis session. Women above the age of 35 comprised 77.77% of the total across all groups, 33.33% of these were over 40. A prominent shift in primary and secondary infertility diagnoses was noted also. Nearly all clients presented with exceptionally high mental/emotional anxieties upon which hypnosis appears to have had a profound effect.

Introduction

Infertility is a serious problem for many women/couples. Infertility patients have very few options as to how they can help themselves. The longer one suffers infertility the worse it becomes as fear, frustration, and despair set in. These, in turn, undermine self-esteem, damage relationships, and destroy hope. Stress levels are high, and emotions are in turmoil. Hypnosis is well-recognized in the literature as the antithesis of stress. Numerous studies indicate the efficacy of hypnosis in the management of many ailments including stress, anxiety, trauma, depression, cancer, and pain control; nearly all of which may accompany fertility struggles.

Infertility assaults the mind/emotions, body, and spirit which can destroy a woman's sense of balance within her life. Women trying to cope with infertility have serious stress levels to contend with, and from numerous contributors including: invasive and/or painful medical tests and procedures, contradictory medical and/or alternative therapy advice, pressure to pursue treatment they have not yet had a chance to process (including adoption and donor eggs), emphasis on a ticking biological clock, questionable statistics promulgated as absolutes, parental pressure to provide grandchildren, and career conflicts. Hypnosis helps to rapidly ease or relieve stress and anxiety levels that may impair the likelihood of conception and/or live birth. Clients report a noticeable difference after just one hypnosis session, whereas they have often been frustrated with meditation attempts, and being told to "just relax" to ease their stress.

Infertility is a growing issue in the United States. According to the Centers for Disease Control and Prevention (CDC), impaired fecundity (impaired ability to get pregnant or carry a baby to term) affects 6.7 million women aged 15 - 44; and 1.5 million married women ages 15 - 44 are infertile (unable to conceive after at least 12 consecutive months of unprotected sex with husband or live-in partner) (CDC, 2015). According to the American Society for Reproductive Medicine (ASRM), infertility affects men and women equally; and there is more than one factor impeding fertility in 25 percent of infertile couples. The male partner is either the contributing or the sole cause of infertility in 40 percent of infertile couples; ovulation issues account for approximately 25 percent of all female infertility problems. Conventional medical therapies such as medication or surgery are used to treat most infertility cases — approximately 85 to 90 percent; in vitro fertilization (IVF), though vital for some patients, accounts for less than three percent of infertility treatment (ASRM, 2015).

A diagnosis of *unexplained infertility* occurs in approximately 25 percent of cases, though these numbers can vary significantly. Unexplained infertility means that there are no apparent medical reasons as to why a woman/couple has not conceived. According to Dr. Richard Sherbahn of the Advanced Fertility Center of Chicago (2017), medical studies have reported that 0 - 26 percent of infertile couples have unexplained infertility, with the most commonly reported figures between 10 and 20 percent. According to Dr. Robert J. Kiltz of CNY Fertility in New York, about 20 - 30 percent of couples will have no definitive diagnosis following a standard infertility workup. The current rate of unexplained infertility, says Dr. Sherbahn, is about 50 percent for couples with a female partner under age 35, and about 80 percent by age 40.

The unexplained infertility diagnosis is a devastating blow for those trying to conceive. This might seem counterintuitive as *un*explained means that a standard infertility evaluation has found *no* medical causes for infertility. However, from the frustrated standpoint of the patient this diagnosis means that nothing can be done — there is no pill, no surgery, no action, no answer. She is no further ahead than she was before she went to the doctor. From the hypnotic standpoint, however, from the hypnotic standpoint, nothing medically wrong is good news. It indicates there may be a psychological issue—a subconscious block of some sort that can be cleared through hypnosis.

In general, persons struggling with infertility not only experience a great deal of suffering from the diagnosis itself, but also from insensitive comments, judgments, lack of support and compassion from others including family and friends, and even a sort of self-imposed social isolation as the issue progresses. There may also be physical and/or emotional trauma from invasive medical procedures and ceaseless rounds of drugs; marital discord caused by emotional and financial stressors; and a spiritual emptiness may emerge as ideas of being punished by God (or client-specified deity), or deemed undeserving, begin to take hold. This presents a unique treatment challenge and underscores the need for additional viable treatment options.

Literature Review

A review of the literature found one recurring theme in particular: the impact of psychological distress in relation to physiological manifestation of infertility. James (2009) found a need to manage psycho-emotional issues which may negatively influence conception, and defines hypnosis as "a deep relaxing technique, reducing stress and the intensity of emotional and psychological concentration." She further states that hypnosis is an effective method to "reduce stress and enhance feelings of control in the mother," and to "manage psycho-emotional issues," such as trauma or body image issues, that may be contributing to infertility (p. 139).

O'Reilly, Sevigny, Sabarre, & Phillips (2014) identified infertility and assisted reproductive technology (ART) as "significant contributors to patients' emotional distress," and those diagnosed with unexplained infertility to be at "particular risk for depression, distress and difficulty reaching acceptance of their infertility" (p. 6). Their article examined the effects of complementary and alternative medicine (CAM) — holistic, non-medical treatments often used in conjunction with ART, or unilaterally as an alternative choice, such as naturopathy, acupuncture, traditional Chinese medicine, and hypnotherapy — for the support and treatment of infertility. According to August (1960), infertility may have an "emotional background," and this emotional impact affects both partners (p. 118).

Levitas, et al. (2006) concluded that the use of hypnosis during the embryo transfer (ET) procedure may significantly improve the cycle outcomes (nearly double the success rate) of IVF/ET cycles with regard to both increased implantation and increased clinical pregnancy rates. This is one of the most prominent studies found in the literature. The objective of this study was to improve both implantation and pregnancy rates through the use of documented hypnosis benefits "such as anxiety and stress reduction" (p. 1404). Levitas, et al. (2006) describe hypnosis as "one of the oldest psychological tools for pain and anxiety relief," drawing support for their research from decades of the well-established and renowned surgical efficacy of hypnosis (p. 1404).

Vyas, Adwanikar, Hathi, & Vyas (2013) "consistently sustained success rates that are unsurpassed" during their 28-year clinical study (p. 169). Thus far, this study appears to be of the longest duration of any on the topic of hypnosis and infertility. There appears to be statistical significance with the overall success rate of 397 pregnancies out of 554, or 71.67 percent (p. 169). According to Vyas, et al. (2013), this result is due to the "insight that psychodynamic tensions can so imbalance the physiology" that, though not revealed by laboratory tests, serve to block fertilization. Hypnosis is the subject of this study, though other psychotherapeutic methods were also employed in some cases.

Literature about the efficacy of hypnosis in direct relation to infertility is scarce, and most of what does exist is decades old. Lack of available recent studies was evidenced, though discovery of an unexpected plethora of early to mid-20th century studies provided a solid background from which to move forward. There is more than one aspect missing from the hypnosis/fertility literature, thus indicating a need to fill in the gaps with carefully constructed, up-to-date research. Overall, the research reviewed indicated that hypnotherapy does help to ease or relieve stress, anxiety, depression issues, and other such contributors to infertility. It further indicates the contemporary need for exploration, to keep with the notion of inquiry versus advocacy, of hypnotherapy as a viable option for the treatment of infertility.

Results

The total combined sample for this study was 36 case files retrieved from the researcher's private practice, and divided into three five-year phases: early, middle, and final developmental cases. Age contributed significantly to the focus of the research because both doctors and patients are concerned with age-related statistics. The currently accepted science is that the older the patient is, the more the likelihood she will have infertility issues. Patients 35 years of age and older are immediately considered high-risk; therefore, it was important to know the ages of the case studies. If the average age of the majority of the case studies was <25 or <30, for example, there would be a greater expectation of fewer fertility issues which would make the impact of hypnosis much more difficult to gauge.

Each of the five-year phases was divided into four age groups for the purpose of evaluating whether or not client age increased with the progression of time and development of the program; overall age did increase significantly across each of the phases. That the age of clients seeking hypnosis assistance increases in the later phases may have something to do with the latest medical technology that makes it possible for women of "advanced maternal age" to become pregnant. It may also reflect the fact that hypnosis to promote fertility has become more readily known. The age percentages of the total across all groups are as follows:

- < 30 = 5.55%

- 30 – 34 = 16.66%

- 35 – 39 = 44.44%

- >40 = 33.33%

Chances for pregnancy and live birth decrease with age, particularly once a woman reaches the age of 35; the older the woman, the less likely she is to conceive (naturally or with medical assistance). The numbers line up as clients above the age of 35 comprise 77.77% of the total across all groups, indicating that women 35 and over need the most assistance.

As the phases progress, there is a steady increase in the age of the clients that would seem to correlate with increases in other categories. Initially, when the researcher began her work with infertility patients, she would estimate a treatment plan of four to six sessions; this is the basis for her first book as well. Somewhere around the second half or so of the second phase the researcher began noticing a longer client duration and began estimating a 12-session average. The overall average number of sessions for the group as a whole was nine sessions per person. In line with prior experience early developmental cases (EDC) averaged four sessions each, middle developmental cases (MDC) averaged 10 sessions each, and final developmental cases (FDC) averaged 13 sessions each. Perhaps this is because of the increased client age, which may also be related to more difficult medical problems. Male factor issues were briefly examined and accounted for 30.55% overall for the entire group. The CDC indicates that contributing and/or exclusive male factor accounts for 40% of infertility issues.

Three elements of the study emerged as the most critical factors. The first is that 88.88% of the entire population were self-diagnosed as Type-A personalities. Synonymous terms included in the 88.88% are perfectionist, control freak, and over achiever. 72.22% specifically used the term Type-A. This type of personality is a "doer," and a doer's stress is seriously increased when she cannot *do* something—because doers can *do* anything. If they want something, they set their minds to it, and they do what it takes to get it. However, a person cannot *do* a baby. No matter how much money, education, intelligence, etc. that a person has she still cannot force a baby to be conceived.

Hypnosis assists this personality type in redirecting their doer abilities into what they *can* do under these circumstances: self-care, making and keeping appointments, initiating IVF if that is their choice, making sure to actually have intercourse if they are trying to conceive naturally. These personalities do not have much patience, and the longer something takes the more stressed over it they become. The purpose of this study was to determine whether or not hypnosis is a viable treatment for infertility, specifically by evaluating the effects of hypnosis on stress, anxiety, and depression that may further impair the likelihood of conception. Countless studies indicate the efficacy of hypnosis for stress, anxiety, and depression; the sheer numbers of self-diagnosed highly stressed individuals indicate the likelihood of this correlation.

The second element is that 100% of infertility patients indicated a significant improvement after their first hypnotherapy session. (100% is a number not typically found in research studies, however as this study was a case review rather than a clinical study, it is included here.) Some said they felt less anxious. Some said they felt more like their old selves. Some expressed feeling less broken. Some more confident. Some said they had never been so relaxed. Some reported that things bothered them less. Many were thrilled that their sex lives had become less regimented already, they were very impressed that they forgot to think about the all-consuming problem ceaselessly, they felt more positive, they reported feeling less frustrated, they felt they had hope once again, etc. Nearly all of these patients had done or were currently doing CAM (complementary and alternative medicine), including acupuncture, yoga and Mayan abdominal massage to help manage stress. Though clients using various forms of CAM found it to be helpful in most cases, each person consistently reported that nothing else had ever helped with their mental/emotional anxiety like hypnosis did.

The third element is the significant shift in the percentages of primary and secondary infertility. According to the World Health Organization (WHO), primary infertility is defined as a woman's inability to ever bear a child due to either the inability to become pregnant *or* the inability to carry a pregnancy through to a live birth. As such, women whose pregnancies miscarry spontaneously or result in a stillborn child—women who have never had a live birth—would be in the primary infertility category along with those who have been unable (thus far) to become pregnant. Secondary infertility is the inability to conceive subsequent to one or more live births. The overall percentages of primary and secondary infertility were 80.55% primary, and 19.44% secondary. In the first phase, 50% of clients had secondary and 50% had primary. By the second phase, clients had 91.66% primary infertility, and 8.33% secondary.

The third phase of clients had 100% primary infertility.

Conclusion

According to the medical specialty known as Reproductive Endocrinology, women ages 35 and up will have a difficult time getting pregnant, and an even more difficult time achieving a healthy pregnancy and live birth. That 77.77% of this study's population were found to be over the age of 35 — consistent with medical findings — and that each one achieved both pregnancy and live birth while undergoing hypnotherapy treatment, appears to be relevant. Based on these findings it would appear that hypnosis is, indeed, a viable treatment for infertility. At the very least, further research is recommended.

References

American Society for Reproductive Medicine (ASRM). (2015). *Quick facts about infertility.*
Retrieved from:
http://www.asrm.org/detail.aspx?id=2322

August, R. V. (1960). Hypnosis: an additional tool in the study of infertility. *Fertility And Sterility 11* 118-123.

CDC/National Center for Health Statistics. (2015). *FastStats.*
Retrieved from:
http://www.cdc.gov/nchs/fastats/infertility.htm

Eastburn, D. (2011). *What is hypnosis? Really.* Westminster, CO: D. James Publishing.

Elkins, G. R., Barabasz, A. F., Council, J. R., & Spiegel, D. (2015). Advancing research and practice: The revised APA Division 30 definition of hypnosis. *International Journal Of Clinical And Experimental Hypnosis, 63*(1), 1-9. doi:10.1080/00207144.2014.961870

Elman, D. (1964). *Hypnotherapy.* Glendale, CA: Westwood Publishing.

Explorable.com. (June, 2009). *Stratified Sampling Method.*
Retrieved Jun 22, 2015 from:
Explorable.com: https://explorable.com/stratified-sampling

James, U. (2009). Practical uses of clinical hypnosis in enhancing fertility, healthy pregnancy and childbirth. *Complementary Therapies In Clinical Practice, 15*(4), 239-241. doi:10.1016/j.ctcp.2009.09.005

Kiltz, R. J. (2017). *Using Laparoscopy to Help Diagnose Unexplained Infertility.*
Retrieved from:
https://www.cnyfertility.com/?s=unexplained+infertility

Levitas, E., Parmet, A., Lunenfeld, E., Bentov, Y., Burstein, E., Friger, M., & Potashnik, G. (2006). Impact of hypnosis during embryo transfer on the outcome of in vitro fertilization-embryo transfer: a case-control study. *Fertility And Sterility, 85*(5), 1404-1408.

Mayo Clinic (2013). *Diseases and conditions: Female infertility treatments and drugs.*

Retrieved from:
http://www.mayoclinic.org/diseases-conditions/female-infertility/basics/treatment/con-20033618

Mayo Clinic (2013). *Tests and procedures: Intrauterine insemination definition.*

Retrieved from:
http://www.mayoclinic.org/tests-procedures/intrauterine-insemination/basics/definition/prc-20018920

Mayo Clinic (2013). *Tests and procedures: In vitro fertilization definition.* Retrieved from:
http://www.mayoclinic.org/tests-procedures/in-vitro-fertilization/basics/definition/prc-20018905

Miller, M. C. (2010). *Unconscious or subconscious?*

Retrieved from:
http://www.health.harvard.edu/blog/unconscious-or-subconscious-20100801255

O'Reilly, E., Sevigny, M., Sabarre, K., & Phillips, K. P. (2014). Perspectives of complementary and alternative medicine (CAM) practitioners in the support and treatment of infertility. *BMC Complementary And Alternative Medicine, 14*394. doi:10.1186/1472-6882-14-394

Sherbahn, R. (2017). *Unexplained Infertility Background, Tests and Treatment Options.*

Retrieved from:

http://www.advancedfertility.com/unexplai.htm

Vyas, R., Adwanikar, G., Hathi, L., & Vyas, B. (2013).
Psychotherapeutic intervention with
hypnosis in 554 couples with reproductive failure. *Journal Of The Indian Medical Association, 111*(3), 167.

World Health Organization (WHO). (2015). *Infertility definitions and terminology.*

Retrieved from:
http://www.who.int/reproductivehealth/topics/infe rtility/definitions/en/

You Are Not Broken

By Lynsi Eastburn, MA, BCH, CI
Originally Published in the NGH HypnoGram Periodical
(2015)

Infertility is a heartbreaking issue that, according to the Centers for Disease Control and Prevention (CDC), affects approximately six percent of married women (15–44 years of age) in the United States alone (2013). Infertility impacts much more than a woman's ability to have a child, and it is not an insignificant matter to be dismissed or discounted. It is a matter that is on par with other catastrophic issues, though it gets less recognition and far less sympathy. In fact, insensitive comments/remarks are the hallmark of this painful journey.

Hypnosis is renowned for its efficacy in stress and anxiety relief (Spiegel, 2013). HypnoFertility® (HF) is a comprehensive application of hypnotic techniques, based on the accepted science, and used to support the many facets of infertility and its treatments. The focus of HF is to elicit a balance of mind/body/spirit, with emphasis on stress relief and ego-strengthening. This assists clients in "taking their lives back," or recovering a sense of normalcy in daily life that enables them to be present, and to enhance positive awareness in other areas of their lives.

There is a consistent theme within the realm of infertility; those enmeshed — particularly women — have essentially resigned to being "broken." By the time a client reaches my office, her self-confidence is shaken, her self-image shattered. An essential focus of HF consultants is to hold the space for a woman to come to terms with this devastating experience. When I say, "hold the space," I am referring to actually hearing (not just listening to) the client, validating her experience, and accepting where she is — sans judgment. Infertility impacts people on multiple levels: it is emotionally, mentally, spiritually, and physically exhausting; and can be financially and socially devastating.

Women who seek my assistance are self-proclaimed Type A personalities, perfectionists, control freaks, over-achievers, etc., so it is no wonder that they have such extreme difficulty in dealing with a problem that cannot be conquered. Over and over I hear the same statement: I have always gotten ANYTHING I set my mind to — except for getting pregnant! I tell clients, students, and readers alike that "you can't left-brain a baby." This statement is key to the utilization of hypnosis to promote fertility — and what led to the development of this specialty.

Society values the intellect, often at the expense of the imagination. This results in a predominance of left-brain thinking — the mainstay of the Type A personality. (For the purpose of this article, terms such as left or right brain, Type A, etc. are consistent with the vernacular, rather than academic terminology.) The left brain is regarded as analytical, decision-making, hard-working, and more or less concrete. The right brain, on the other hand, is considered imaginative, creative, day-dreamy, abstract. That the scientist is left-brained, and the artist is right-brained is a common notion; the fact is, we need both. Time Magazine (1999) proclaims Albert Einstein to be the "preeminent scientist" of the 20th century, though Einstein himself—in a 1929 issue of The Saturday Evening Post—says: "I am enough of the artist to draw freely upon my imagination. Imagination is more important than knowledge. Knowledge is limited. Imagination encircles the world" (p. 117).

HF clients rely on their intellect, on their innate ability to achieve whatever they put their minds to. They are "do-ers" (left brain) and the concept of "being" (right brain) is often incomprehensible to them. Discussion of the necessity of receptivity, of surrender, of allowing; in other words of "being," elicits the response of okay, how do I DO that?! or I do everything they say, exactly the way they say to do it, and I still can't get pregnant! "They" being reproductive endocrinologists (RE), naturopathic doctors (ND), acupuncturists, nutritionists, and other assorted fertility consultants. There is a quandary here: often these professionals contradict each other.

Though often unknown to patients, RE protocols vary significantly on a global basis. What might be standard assisted reproductive technology (ART) practice at one US clinic may differ completely from the standards of foreign clinics, from one state to the next, and even from one local clinic to another. Recommended diets vary significantly not only from one modality to another, but within each modality. For example, women are told that some alcohol is fine but to never have caffeine; or that caffeine is okay, but alcohol is forbidden; or that they must take Chinese herbs; or to avoid Chinese herbs at all costs; they must eat/must avoid red meat; eat raw vegetables/eat only cooked vegetables... Sugar and gluten are pretty consistently "evil," but dealing with so many contradictions is exceptionally frustrating.

I describe HF as the "missing link" because it supports all modalities without contradiction. Unlike any other practitioners our clients may encounter, HF consultants can validate their experiences because we are not invested in any outcome. We have no agenda. HF is designed to facilitate the healing of debilitating "brokenness;" it helps to relieve fear and confusion; and it fosters a healthy mind state where all other factors can be effectively evaluated, integrated, or discarded as appropriate.

Our job is not to contradict medical advice; nor is it to dispute anything else our clients may be doing. We can be of most service by helping them to reclaim the balance necessary to discern which direction or treatment is right for them, without constant second-guessing or self-deprecation. This is what I refer to as the "balance of intention and surrender." Through HF, clients are able to be present in the moment, and to undergo any treatment or procedure without pre-conceived "certainties" of failure. They are not only validated but empowered; they experience a restoration of mind/body/spirit balance, and a sense of "normalcy" in their everyday lives. Because of HypnoFertility®, our clients know they are not broken.

   *Note: men and/or couples are also impacted by infertility; to maintain simplicity I have referred only to women here.

This article was written for a hypnotherapy organization and is, therefore, more therapist-focused. I thought there might be some bits in it that you could use, so I am including it here.

THE CHEESE STANDS ALONE

By Lynsi Eastburn, MA, BCH, CI

The Farmer in the Dell is an old German nursery rhyme that dates back to the early 19th century. It is an often-played children's game where a group of children form a circle and sing an ongoing song. The song, verse by verse, details the acquisition of a person by the preceding person, with an implied sequence of the subsequent characters' declining standing. The farmer begins the game from the center of the circle. The farmer takes a wife. Next, the wife takes a child. The child then takes a nurse, and so on, until eventually there is only one child left unchosen. This child is designated the cheese, and the cheese stands alone.

The farmer in the dell, the farmer in the dell, hi ho the derry-o the farmer in the dell…
The farmer takes a wife, the farmer takes a wife, hi ho the derry-o the farmer takes a wife…

I always thought *The Farmer in the Dell* to be a cruel game for children, as it is really nothing more than a popularity contest that leaves the quiet child, the different child, the unchosen child feeling even more ostracized than usual. That same sentiment is experienced by infertile women as others all around them become pregnant without apparent difficulty, while they themselves cannot. An already delicate situation—the inability to conceive—is exacerbated, their already glaring lack is underscored by those who are seemingly chosen by Nature. This cruelty is cast, perhaps most perceptibly, upon the last woman remaining in any so-called support group.

The infertility issue does not lend itself well to the whole support group concept, despite the desperate need most women have to be part of one, to receive some kind of compassion and understanding from others experiencing similar difficulties. The children's game continues until everyone has been picked but one person. Even the rat — considered a loathsome creature by the general populace — has been taken. The last person — the cheese — is excluded from the group, is not chosen (not pregnant), is (must be) lower than even a rat.

The cheese stands alone, the cheese stands alone, hi ho the derry-o the cheese stands alone.

Within fertility "support" groups, the same thing happens. As each woman conceives (is chosen), she leaves. Just as relief floods each child as she is plucked from the ever-diminishing circle — her place secured — the now pregnant woman no longer wants any part of the infertility nightmare; she wants to move on to the next stage of her life. Just as children may feel sorry for the classmate who remains alone, ultimately, they are grateful not to be that person. And so it is with each newly pregnant woman. The support group is a reminder of the nightmare that she no longer has to endure, she has been chosen.

One by one the group members get pregnant, and one by one—just as fewer children remain in the circle—the other members are left; feeling abandoned, feeling like they don't matter. Each pregnancy metes more suffering than the previous as the group dwindles. Until there is one woman left. That very last woman stands alone. She now "knows" that she is the outcast, that she is the one hated by God, that she is worthless, that she is nothing.

Abandonment chips the cheese's soul in increments; with each chorus, someone else is chosen. (Why won't anyone pick me?) *The Farmer in the Dell* is an excellent metaphor for what women trying to conceive must endure as one after another, after another, of their friends, relatives, colleagues— and even strangers—get pregnant before they do. And within the confines of the "support" group, where all members are there for the same reason, each confirmed pregnancy is that much harder to bear. In the "real" world, such incidents might be infrequent, or easier to avoid. But there is no escaping the inevitable exclamations of yet another happily-ever- after from within the group. And with every one, confidence is diminished. Eventually, there is nothing left but the endless sense of brokenness.

Not everyone understands the infertility issue, and not everyone cares about it. I have had women in my office who confess that at one time they dismissed other women's pain as a virtual non-issue, that they couldn't fathom what these women were "whining" about. Now as these women sit with me, tears streaming, sobs retching, they are faced with the guilt of being unsupportive to a friend in a time of need, and — because they are now in the same situation — feeling punished because (in their minds) of the "karma" being dealt to them for their previous lack of sensitivity. And "no one cares." And now they get it.

The infertility struggle triggers countless self-punishment programs in a woman's life. She is at fault because she cannot conceive, she is at fault because she waited too long, she is at fault because her eggs are too old, she is at fault because she wanted a career, she is at fault because of a previous abortion; the list is endless. For all of these infractions — and more — she must be punished. Old wounds are gouged open, deep wounds that have been suppressed — not addressed, not healed — will no longer remain contained. Unbridled angst bursts through the surface of the psyche; an excruciating journey begins.

The symbolism found in this children's rhyme may be interpreted in many ways. The patriarchal hierarchy is immediately apparent as the farmer, who is clearly the key player (one might say *the big cheese*) in the game, becomes the owner or possessor of all that come after him. He is the director, everyone else must follow his course. The infertility issue has a similar layout. There is a very masculine energy dominating the reproductive medicine arena—a more aggressive, directive, top-down progression than an inclusive, holistic, feminine approach.

I am not talking male/female, but rather the associated, archetypal energies of the so-called masculine and feminine forces. For example: hard/soft, expansive/contractive, yang/yin, light/dark, and sympathetic/parasympathetic, respectively.

Women often end up feeling left out, discounted, and even abandoned. The body is separated from the self, the soul. The mind, body, spirit unity is disconnected in favor of unilateral impregnation—whatever the cost.

The feminine is not to be excluded, however, as it is a circle that the children form around the farmer. The circle represents the power of the female, as well as completion or wholeness. It is the Earth Mother, it is sacred space. A dell may be defined as a secluded hollow, a ravine, a shallow terra valley nestled amidst the trees.

A ravine may also be described as a chasm, an abyss. These terms may bring to mind a sense of struggle, or of facing a seemingly insurmountable obstacle or subconscious block; a fear of the unknown, of losing control, of loss, even an infinite emptiness. A hollow, or cave, represents the womb, the Earth Mother. Rebirth or transition often takes place in a cave. Terra means earth or ground. The

Roman Goddess of the Earth is known as Terra — a fertility deity. The archetypal World Tree, also known as the Tree of Life or the Tree of Knowledge, connects the earth, the heavens, and the underworld. As above, so below. And so it is written.

The cheese stands alone in the dell — virtually abandoned in the abyss. Or so it would seem. But the cheese is not alone. She is encircled by the goddess, protected by the Earth Mother. The cheese is not alone.

AFTERWORD

*"Refusal of the summons converts
the adventure into its negative."*
— Joseph Campbell

I am living my Dharma. I am walking my path. I am embracing my journey. As are you. In *Depth Psychology* this is the process of *individuation* — the psychological and conscious emergence of the *Self* — originally defined and identified by Carl Jung. The world-renowned mythologist, Joseph Campbell, refers to it as *the call to adventure* or *the hero's journey* that each of us, in some way, must respond to. Even not responding is, in effect, responding; as to ignore or suppress one's soul's deepest yearnings is to respond with indifference to — and invalidation of — the *Self*, to ignore its cries, and to snuff its raison d'être (reason to be) before it can ever breach the surface of the psyche.

Just as the mythical phoenix, in rising from its ashes, inspires many to carry on even in the direst of circumstances, so is our calling meant to inspire growth, and encourage us toward transcendence. Each and every one of us has an individual journey to pursue, though we may or may not choose to undertake it. Ideally, in completing the journey, we acquire a wholeness that encompasses every lesson and every experience encountered along the way.

To me, the individuation process is life itself; and as I consider my own, I recognize the various mini-journeys or rites of passage contained within. It is my personal experience that in yielding to the progression, without trying to intellectualize, each phenomenon is observed and expressed, archetypes freed, symbolism unleashed, the confines of the psyche suddenly not so confining. Such is the balance of intention and surrender. Such is trusting the journey. And is that not, ultimately, its purpose?

Fertility troubles are a gift—though it may not seem that way right now. They are an initiation, a rite of passage that you will endure, and transcend. And you will be better for it. Because of this experience you are learning to let go, and to find and maintain balance within your life. Your children will benefit significantly from your struggles, your strength. And you will truly know your *Self*.

I am privileged to help bring babies into this world. To be able to spend my moments doing what I love is a wondrous gift that I hold sacred in my heart. I humbly offer gratitude to the Universe for the opportunity to fulfill my calling in this way. I trust that the information, thoughts, references, articles, and case studies contained within will serve to inspire you, and bring you hope.

NAMASTÉ

PRIVATE HYPNOFERTILITY® CLIENTS

I do work with private clients in-office, by telephone (Facetime, Facebook Messenger, etc.), and via video-conferencing programs such as *Zoom* and *Skype*. I am currently accepting new clients on a limited basis. Please contact my office if you are interested in working directly with me.

LYNSI EASTBURN, MA
HYPNOFERTILITY INTERNATIONAL
Westminster, CO
303-424-2331
office@hypnodenver.com
www.hypnofertility.com
www.spiritbabywhisperer.com

PREMIER HYPNOFERTILITY® THERAPISTS

Following is a list of my preferred network of HypnoFertility® experts. This group consists of Certified HypnoFertility® Therapists with whom I have a first-hand and ongoing relationship. These are the people I feel I can personally recommend. With the ease of distance communication through video conferencing programs such as *Skype*, there is no longer a need for local referrals. What is needed is serious, dedicated, professional HF therapists who are actively practicing and/or establishing their practices. *In alphabetical order…*

DEE BALLINGTON, MA, LOACC, CH, CHFC

Certified HypnoFertility® Consultant, *Eastburn Institute of Hypnosis*

Certified Hypnotherapist, *Quantum Edge Healing Institute*

Law of Attraction Certified Life Coach, *Quantum Success Coaching Academy*

Master of Arts, *New York University*

HYPNO FERTILITY SOLUTIONS

32 North Sunnycrest Drive
Little Silver, NJ 07739
Phone: 1-732-615-8368
Website: www.hypnofertilitysolutions.com
E-mail: dee@hypnofertilitysolutions.com
Facebook: Hypno Fertility Solutions
Skype: Dee Ballington

***

LISA BRENT, MA, CH

Certified HypnoFertility® Therapist

CALLING HARMONY HYPNOTHERAPY

1660 S. Albion Street
Denver, CO
80222
Phone: 1-303-551-1989
Website: www.callingharmony.com

***

ANITA BUTLER, BA–IBCLC, CCHT, HBCE, CPD (DONA)

Certified HypnoFertility® Therapist
Renegade tamer of birth fears, postpartum overwhelm, and breastfeeding bugaboos — oh, my!

SACRED SEASON MOTHER CARE
IN ASSOCIATION WITH BIRTH EDUCATION CENTER OF SAN DIEGO

9845 Erma Rd.
San Diego, CA 92131
Phone: 1-916-524-1080
Website: www.sacredseasonmothercare.com
Website: www.birtheducationcenter.com
E-mail: anita@sacredseasonmothercare.com

***

MELANIE COLWELL

Registered Professional Clinical Hypnotherapist
Certified HypnoFertility® Practitioner
NLP Practitioner
Certified Eating Psychology and Mind-Body
Nutrition Coach, Pilates Instructor

MELANIE COLWELL FERTILITY COACHING

Adelaide, South Australia
Consults worldwide via Skype
Phone: +61 404 488 952
Website: www.melaniecolwell.com

***

KEN DOMBROWSKI, CH
Certified HypnoFertility® Therapist
Master Hypnotist

LOVE YOUR LIFE HYPNOSIS
2701 Larsen Rd #115
Green Bay, WI 54303
Phone: 1-920-412-9980
Website: www.loveyourlifehypnosis.com

***

NANCY J. DOUGLAS, CI, CH, CNLP, HBCOMM
Consulting Hypnotist & NGH Certified Instructor
Certified HypnoFertility® Therapist

HALTON HYPNOSIS CENTRE & SCHOOL
3425 Harvester Rd.,
Suite 207
Burlington, Ontario
Canada
L7N3N1
Phone: 1-905-516-2234
Website: www.haltonhypnosis.com
Website: www.CanadianHypnoFertility.com

***

VERONICA GIANNINI, CH
Certified Hypnotist
Certified HypnoFertility® Therapist

IVF STRESS RELIEF
2977 Coconut Ave.
Coconut Grove, FL 33133
Phone: 1-347-549-2659
Website: ivfstressrelief.com

***

ALANNA JACKSON, CH
Certified Consulting Hypnotist - National Guild of
Hypnotists
Certified HypnoFertility® Therapist
Certified 5-PATH® Hypnotherapist
Certified 7th Path Self-Hypnosis® Teacher
PSYCH-K® Facilitator

HYPNOTIC RESOLUTIONS
1590 Atkinson Rd., Ste 102
Lawrenceville, GA 30043
Phone: 1-678-983-8686
Website: www.HypnoticResolutions.com
E-mail: Info@hypnoticresolutions.com

***

ADRIANNE LATIMOUR, MCHT, MTLT, MNLP, HBCE
Clinic Owner
Certified HypnoFertility® Therapist
Master Level Hypnotherapist
Coach

DYNAMIC HEALTH THERAPY INC.
24018 Woodbine Avenue
Keswick, Ontario, Canada
Phone: 1-905-535-3330
Website: www.KeswickTherapy.com
E-mail: info@DynamicHealthTherapy.com

***

SHERRIE MARTIN, MA, CH
Certified Hypnotherapist
Certified HypnoFertility® Therapist
Successful HypnoFertility® Client!

FLATIRONS HYPNOTHERAPY
80 Garden Center, STE 154
Broomfield, CO 80020
Phone: 1-720 445-9848
Website: flatirons hypnotherapy.com

***

AYALON SHEREFKIN
Certified Hypnotherapist
Certified HypnoFertility®
Certified Hypnocoach
Master Practitioner NLP & Guided Imagination

NIKLATLI – SUBCONTIOUS FERTILITY
Bonei Hair 9, Tel Aviv
Phone: 052-363-3391
Website: www.niklatli.co.il
E-mail: NiklatLi1@gmail.com

***

WAKABA NAKAMURA TAITANO
Certified Clinical Hypnotherapist
Certified HypnoFertility® Therapist

BODY & MIND
Guam USA
and
Nagano Japan
Phone: +1 (671) 988-1119 / +81 (050) 5534-0417
Website: www.bodyandmindguam.com

***

68209759R10102

Made in the USA
Columbia, SC
05 August 2019